EDITED BY
GERARD MCCANN, NITA MISHRA AND
PÁDRAIG CARMODY

WITH A FOREWORD
BY COLM BROPHY

COVID-19, THE GLOBAL SOUTH AND THE PANDEMIC'S DEVELOPMENT IMPACT

BRISTOL
UNIVERSITY
PRESS

First published in Great Britain in 2022 by

Bristol University Press
University of Bristol
1–9 Old Park Hill
Bristol
BS2 8BB
UK
t: +44 (0)117 374 6645
e: bup-info@bristol.ac.uk

Details of international sales and distribution partners are available at bristoluniversitypress.co.uk

British Library Cataloguing in Publication Data
A catalogue record for this book is available from the British Library

ISBN 978-1-5292-2565-5 paperback
ISBN 978-1-5292-2566-2 OA ePub
ISBN 978-1-5292-2567-9 OA ePdf

Cover design: Bristol University Press
Front cover image: RomeoLu – iStock.com
Bristol University Press use environmentally responsible print partners.
Printed and bound in Great Britain by CMP, Poole

Contents

List of Figures and Tables   vi

List of Abbreviations   vii

Notes on Contributors   ix

Foreword   xv
Colm Brophy

Introduction   1
Gerard McCann, Nita Mishra and Pádraig Carmody

PART I Perspectives and Theory

one   Surviving Necropolitical Developments amid   9
Democratic Disinformation: A Pandemic
Perspective from Brazil
Su-ming Khoo and Mayara Floss

two   COVID-19, International Development and   24
the Global Economy
Stephen McCloskey and Amit Prakash

three   Global Finance and the COVID-19 Pandemic   38
in Africa
Howard Stein and Rick Rowden

four   COVID-19 Vaccine Inequality and Global   56
Development: A Primer
Rory Horner

PART II Policy Context

five   Corporate Social Responsibility in the Time   77
            of Pandemic: An Indian Overview
            Sujay Ghosh and Naveen Das

six   Local Community and Policy Solutions to a   93
            Global Pandemic
            Pieternella Pieterse

seven   Pandemic Structure and Blowback: 104
            Endemic Inequality and the New (ab)Normal
            Pádraig Carmody and Gerard McCann

eight   Ending a Pandemic   117
            Zeke Ngcobo and Thomas Pogge

PART III Regional and Community Responses

nine   Coping Mechanisms of Communities in   131
            Odisha: A Human Rights-Based Approach
            to the COVID-19 Pandemic
            *Nita Mishra, Sushree Sailani Suman and
            Anuradha Mohanty*

ten   To Lockdown or Not to Lockdown: A   149
            Pragmatic Policy Response to COVID-19
            in Zambia
            Chrispin Matenga and Munguzwe Hichambwa

eleven   Latin America: Politics in Times of COVID-19   162
            *Salvador Martí i Puig and Manuel
            Alcántara Sáez*

twelve   Vietnam's Response to the COVID-19   181
            Pandemic
            *Edward Lahiff, Pham Quang Minh and
            Nguyễn Trọng Chính*

CONTENTS

Conclusion   197
Ashok Acharya

Index   201

List of Figures and Tables

Figures
3.1   MVA as a percentage of GDP for South   43
       Korea and Sub-Saharan Africa, 1960–2020
4.1   Share of people vaccinated against   62
       COVID-19, 18 April 2022
4.2   COVID-19 vaccine doses administered   63
       per 100 people, by income group

Tables
3.1   Personal remittances, ODA and FDI in   45
       SSA 1990–2019 ($ millions)
3.2   SSA sovereign bond issues excluding   48
       South Africa, millions of USD, 2006–21
3.3   Chinese lending to African governments   50
       and state-owned enterprises
5.1   CSR activities of Indian corporates   87
11.1   COVID-19 key dates and number of   164
       deaths in Latin America
11.2   Government communications in   166
       response to the COVID-19 crisis
11.3   Institutional leadership during the   172
       COVID-19 crisis
11.4   Level of involvement of political and   174
       social actors in the COVID-19 crisis

List of Abbreviations

ACT	Access to COVID-19 Tools
Africa CDC	Africa Centres for Disease Control and Prevention
ASHA	Accredited Service Health Workers
AVAT	Africa Vaccine Acquisitions Trust
AWW	Anganwadi Workers
COVAX	COVID-19 Vaccines Global Access Facility
CSR	Corporate Social Responsibility
DSAI	Development Studies Association Ireland
EYN	Ecosavers Youth Network
FDI	foreign direct investment
GAVI	Global Alliance for Vaccines and Immunisation
GDP	gross domestic product
GFC	global financial crisis
HIC	high-income countries
HIF	Health Impact Fund
HIV/AIDS	human immunodeficiency virus/acquired immunodeficiency syndrome
IMF	International Monetary Fund
LICs	low-income countries
LMICs	low- and middle-income countries
MGNREGA	Mahatma Gandhi National Rural Employment Guarantee Act
MSF	Médecins Sans Frontières
MVA	manufacturing value added
NGO	nongovernmental organizations
ODA	overseas development aid
OECD	Organisation for Economic Co-operation and Development
PDS	public distribution system
PECUC	People's Cultural Centre

PF	Patriotic Front
PPE	personal protective equipment
R&D	research and development
RECOVERY	Randomised Evaluation of Covid-19 Therapy
SHGs	self-help groups
SII	Serum Institute of India
SSA	Sub-Saharan African
SUS	Sistema Único de Saúde
SWAN	Stranded Workers Action Network
TB	tuberculosis
TRIPS	Trade-Related Aspects of Intellectual Property Rights
UNCTAD	United Nations Conference on Trade and Development
UNDP	United Nations Development Programme
UNICEF	United Nations Children's Fund
UPND	United Party for National Development
WHO	World Health Organization

Notes on Contributors

Amit Prakash is Professor of Law and Governance at the Jawaharlal Nehru University, New Delhi, India. His areas of research include the politics of development and identity; critical governance studies (including governance indicators); conflict, governance and the state; the democratic political process in India; policing in India; and global governance.

Anuradha Mohanty is Executive Director of NGO People's Cultural Centre, Odisha, India. She was a member of the Juvenile Justice Board, Khordha, from 2010 to 2019 with additional responsibilities for Nayagarh district from 2017 to 2018. She is also a member of the Odisha State Social Security Board for unorganized workers. Her book *Lockdown Diaries* was published in 2020.

Ashok Acharya is Professor of Political Science and leads the Program on Global Justice at the Delhi School of Transnational Affairs, University of Delhi. He was previously Henry Hart Rice Visiting Associate Professor in Global Justice and South Asian Studies at Yale's MacMillan Center. He holds a PhD in political science from the University of Toronto. His research interests lie in contemporary political theory, including issues of social justice, diversity and rights of groups; comparative enquiries in political philosophy; and cosmopolitan ethics and politics.

Chrispin Matenga holds a PhD in development studies and is a lecturer and researcher in the Department of Development Studies at the University of Zambia. His research focuses on agrarian studies, food systems and rural livelihoods. He has published extensively in rural development in Sub-Saharan Africa.

Edward Lahiff is Lecturer in International Development at University College Cork, Ireland. He has previously worked in Southern Africa with a rural NGO and later as Senior Lecturer in Land and Agrarian Studies at the University of the Western Cape. In 2009–10, he served as Doctoral Programme Officer with the Trinity International Development Initiative and Coordinator of the International Doctoral School in Global Health at the Centre for Global Health, Trinity College Dublin. He has published widely on land reform, rural livelihoods and natural resources in Africa, on links between agriculture and nutrition and on migration in South East Asia.

Gerard McCann is Senior Lecturer in International Studies and Head of International Programmes at St Mary's University College, a College of Queen's University Belfast. He is Visiting Professor at the Jagiellonian University, Kraków. He has worked extensively in Sub-Saharan Africa and Eastern Europe. His most recent book is the co-edited *International Human Rights, Social Policy and Global Development* (Policy Press, 2020). He specializes in the European Union's development policy, international relations and economic development.

Howard Stein is Professor in Afro-American and African Studies and Epidemiology at the University of Michigan. He is a development economist educated in Canada, the United States and the UK and has held appointments at universities and research institutes in Japan, the Netherlands, UK, Canada, Ireland, Tanzania and Portugal.

Manuel Alcántara Sáez holds a doctorate in political science from the Complutense University of Madrid. He is Professor of Political Science at the University of Salamanca. His areas of specialization include Latin American politics, comparative politics, elections, political parties and party systems.

Mayara Floss is a PhD graduate and research assistant at the *Departamento de patologia da Faculdade de Medicina da USP* São Paulo, Brazil. She founded the programme of Popular Education 'Health Education League' and coordinated the project until 2014. In 2014, she received a scholarship from the Brazilian government to complete a fellowship on the program Science without Borders at National University of Ireland, Galway.

Munguzwe Hichambwa is a socioeconomic development consultant who worked for 16 years as Business Development Manager at the Indaba Agricultural Policy Research Institute in Zambia. He is currently a senior consultant and managing partner at IPOMEA CONSULT in Lusaka, Zambia.

Naveen Das is Professor and Dean, School of Business and Economics, and Pro-Vice Chancellor, Adamas University, Kolkata, India. In his academic experience, he has held the positions of Founding Dean and Director, IBS Business School, at both Hyderabad and Kolkata, and had a stint as Associate Director, Indian School of Business, Hyderabad, before serving NSHM Knowledge Campus, Kolkata, as Director, School of Business and Management.

Nguyễn Trọng Chính is a postgraduate researcher at the Faculty of International Studies, University of Social Sciences and Humanities, Vietnam National University, Hanoi.

Nita Mishra is a lecturer in International Development at the University of Limerick, Ireland. Her research interests lie with human rights-based approaches to development, gender and empowerment, feminist research methodologies, community-based organizations, migration, and peace studies. She is the Chair of Development Studies Association Ireland.

Pádraig Carmody is Professor in Geography at Trinity College Dublin and Senior Research Associate at the University of Johannesburg. He is currently an associate editor of the journal *Transnational Corporations*, published by the United Nations Conference on Trade and Development and member of the Standing Committee on International Affairs of the Royal Irish Academy. He formerly chaired the Steering Committee of the Development Studies Association of Ireland and is director of the Masters in Development Practice at Trinity College Dublin.

Pham Quang Minh is Professor of History and Politics, and Chair of the Department of International Development Studies at the Faculty of International Studies, University of Social Sciences and Humanities, Vietnam National University, Hanoi.

Pieternella Pieterse is a postdoctoral researcher at Dublin City University, School of Nursing, Psychotherapy and Community Health. She is working on COALESCE-funded research focusing on infant feeding policy implementation in Malawi. Prior to this, she spent eight years in Ethiopia and Tanzania working for research projects and UN agencies such as the Ethiopian Social Accountability Programme, Making all Voices Count (IDS, Sussex University), the World Bank and UNICEF. In 2019, Pieternella conducted research for UNICEF in Ethiopia's Somali Region, examining health budget decision-making and funding flows at district level.

Rick Rowden is Adjunct Professorial Lecturer in the School of International Service at American University and a senior economist at the Washington, DC-based research NGO, Global Financial Integrity. He recently completed his PhD on India–Africa economic relations in the Centre for Economic Studies and Planning at Jawaharlal Nehru University in New Delhi. His academic areas of specialization are international relations, international political economy and development economics. Previously, he has worked for international development NGOs and the United Nations Conference on Trade and Development in Geneva.

Rory Horner is Senior Lecturer in Globalization and Political Economy at the University of Manchester's Global Development Institute and Senior Research Associate at the University of Johannesburg's Department of Geography, Environmental Management and Energy Studies. His research focuses on the political economy of globalization and the pharmaceutical industry.

Salvador Martí i Puig holds a doctorate in political science from the Autonomous University of Barcelona. He is Professor of Political Science at the University of Girona. His areas of specialization include Latin American politics, democratization and de-democratization, social movements and collective action, and political parties.

Stephen McCloskey is the Director of the Centre for Global Education, a development nongovernmental organization in Belfast that provides training and resources on international development issues. He is the editor of *Policy and Practice: A Development Education Review*, a bi-annual journal. His latest book is *Global Learning and International Development in the Age of Neoliberalism* (Routledge, 2022).

Sujay Ghosh is Associate Professor of Political Science, Vidyasagar University, Midnapore. He previously worked at Uluberia College, affiliated to the University of Calcutta, as Associate Professor. His specialist interests are Indian politics, democracy and citizenship, and political education.

Su-ming Khoo is Senior Lecturer in the School of Political Science and Sociology, National University of Ireland Galway.

She is Cluster Leader of the Whitaker Institute: Environment, Development and Sustainability, and the Ryan Institute: Socio-Economic Impact Research Clusters at NUI Galway. She holds a PhD in Sociology and Social Policy from Queen's University Belfast.

Sushree Sailani Suman has a master's in biotechnology from Utkal University, Odisha. She has nearly a decade of experience in writing and editing research articles. She is active in the field of social work. Sushree volunteers with many nongovernmental organizations developing content for their websites and social media pages, and as a trainer for youth on various social and environmental issues. She is currently working as Team Lead at Contentmakers.in.

Thomas Pogge received his PhD in philosophy from Harvard University, is Leitner Professor of Philosophy and International Affairs and founding Director of the Global Justice Program at Yale. He co-founded Academics Stand Against Poverty, an international network aiming to enhance the impact of scholars, teachers and students on global poverty. He is also a co-founder of Incentives for Global Health, a team effort towards creating new incentives that would improve access to advanced pharmaceuticals worldwide.

Zeke Ngcobo received her master's in public health at Sahmyook University in South Korea. She has launched a website called All Things Public Health that is dedicated to the dissemination of accurate information on matters pertaining to public health. She currently works with the Health Impact Fund as the Regional Coordinator for Sub-Saharan Africa.

Foreword

Colm Brophy, TD

Minister of State for Overseas Development Aid and Diaspora

Dublin, 2022

We have all discovered that it is quite something to live through a pandemic. Each one of us was impacted, some more directly than others, no matter where we lived. Thankfully, through clever science and hard work, including by the development system, we have moved to a new phase. At home, life is becoming more normal, as it is elsewhere. Travel is opening up, and we, once again, can walk with others and understand better their lived realities.

Those realities reveal a world that is under strain, with increasing demand for development and humanitarian investments – among others – but with many countries' economies still strained by the impact of COVID lockdowns, reduced tax takes, increased expenditures, supply chain disruptions, inflation and conflict.

Although things are better than they were in 2020, we cannot be complacent about COVID. This phase of the pandemic is playing out very differently across continents, across countries and across communities. There are still pockets with high case numbers. Vaccine hesitancy remains high in many countries, increasing the risk of another variant. We must still be vigilant.

The pandemic has reminded us that we need to reinvest in achieving the Sustainable Development Goals (SDGs). Delivering on this shared global agenda will help address many of the underlying drivers that magnified the impact of COVID-19 for many of the poorest people in the world. Delivering on the SDGs everywhere will also make us safer at home.

I am particularly conscious, though, that there is ground to be made up. The essential focus on the immediate pandemic response held back, and in some cases reversed, progress towards achieving the SDGs.

Investment in global public health systems will help address maternal and child mortality. It will help roll out universal vaccination campaigns, protecting people from childhood and, as we have learned, adult diseases. We can eradicate some diseases – we have come so close with polio. We can make greater progress tackling HIV/AIDS, TB and malaria. In leading the Irish Aid response to the pandemic, I have consistently championed the need to respond to COVID by strengthening health systems, maintaining emphases also on the wider disease burden that countries must address as well as on ensuring that the health needs of the most marginalized and vulnerable are prioritized.

I have also prioritized the deepening of Irish Aid support for education. The closing of schools for public health reasons has had many unintended but difficult consequences. With their education interrupted, millions of children, particularly girls, are now unlikely to return to school. Many teachers have sought other jobs. Investment now will help mitigate the impacts – which in too many cases will be intergenerational, as girls are marrying while still teenagers and having babies at a very young age. Indices of domestic and gender-based violence rose during the pandemic, including at home, which needs considered responses. Ireland's focus on girls' education, and education in emergencies, is helping to address these inequalities and overcome them.

Against a backdrop of increased pressure on household livelihoods and diets, in part due to the pandemic but also due to conflict and climate, 2021 was a year of unprecedented focus on sustainable food systems. Ireland took leadership positions at two major UN summits, on food systems and nutrition, to help focus attention on what needs to be done to address underlying causes of hunger. However, since then, the Russian invasion of Ukraine has further complicated global food security. As an elected member of the UN Security Council, Ireland has led on hunger and conflict, to help create conditions for an improved system response to these interlinked challenges. This will help alleviate pressure on a humanitarian system struggling to meet the increased need as the long tail effects of the pandemic play out.

I am proud of Ireland's record as a consistent, reliable and impartial humanitarian donor. In leading Irish Aid, I want us to constantly strive to make the humanitarian system ever more effective. Later this year, I will launch a new civil society funding mechanism that will help ensure Irish NGOs are best supported in their humanitarian mandate, while also working along the continuum into development.

In 2022, Ireland's development cooperation programme will exceed €1 billion for the very first time. The Irish government's response to the pandemic has been driven throughout by a focus on the effectiveness of multilateral institutions and processes, and the need to focus on the furthest behind first, as originally stated in *A Better World*, Ireland's policy for international development.

As we intensify our efforts across food systems, nutrition, health, education and climate change, I am acutely aware of the unique contribution that Irish researchers and professionals make in these and other areas. Irish Aid funding means nothing if it is not accompanied by Irish expertise, empathy and partnership. Members of the Development Studies Association Ireland (DSAI) are vital in this effort, seeking to share Irish experience and expertise with counterparts, and, indeed, help Ireland learn from experiences elsewhere.

This volume serves as a timely reminder that the pandemic is far from over, and that the challenge of addressing the development losses that resulted from it is only now beginning. We are also reminded that the other global threat of our generation – climate change – has not gone away. We need to retain our focus on delivering on the Paris Agreement, particularly with those most affected and least responsible for climate change firmly in our sights.

The important research collected here, along with the previous volume from the DSAI, drawn from their work throughout the pandemic, highlights how the turbulence of the pandemic has impacted on developing countries – and particularly the most vulnerable and marginalized people. Now is a time to reset, take stock and redouble our efforts.

Key to this will be effective global engagement through our development cooperation programme and active partnership with governments, civil society and the multilateral system. We must leverage effective, multidisciplinary global research and learning carried out by academics and practitioners in Ireland. The DSAI's role as a 'home' for such researchers and cutting-edge expertise is vital. They facilitate vital learning and sharing across practitioners, policymakers and the voices and experience of those on the ground. I am delighted to continue this close collaboration and wish the DSAI and its members every success in future research and learning efforts.

Introduction

Gerard McCann, Nita Mishra and Pádraig Carmody

Going into a third year of the COVID-19 pandemic and with fourth and fifth waves affecting international development in myriad ways, reflection and analysis on what has been happening is continually needed. The pandemic developed at differing paces across diverse contexts around the world and elicited quite disparate societal reactions to what has been the biggest global health emergency in a century. Even a cursory glance at the data on the spread of the virus reveals that governments in all contexts were ill-prepared for the emergence of such a virulent pathogen, its spread and severity. Registering a death toll of over 6 million people and more than 500 million cases by the summer of 2022, the history of this pandemic has been determined primarily by the patterns of contagion, emerging variants, often erratic political decision-making and by inequalities in healthcare and pharmaceutical provision.

For the Global South, the pandemic has served to further expose the gross imbalances in health systems, the recoiling protectionism of the Global North and, ultimately, a residual inflexibility in power relations that has unnecessarily left many highly vulnerable regions open to the worst effects of the virus. There is a need to critically reflect on the reactions and responses to the pandemic so that policymakers, in particular, can be more fully informed about the social, economic, political, security and healthcare implications of this globalized event and plan for the future. There is also a need to survey the socioeconomic effects of this pandemic on low-income countries, and to seek corrections to the prevailing patterns of power and governance that have exacerbated its impacts.

Governmental responses have been critical in dealing with the fall-out and indeed in adapting to the different variants. In some cases, state reactions have brought into question the very principle of protecting public well-being. This, arguably, has been one of the most revealing aspects of this period – affecting international development, policy and practice alike. There remain many countries, most notably but not exclusively in the Global South, without the requisite resources, professionals, political acumen or international weight to cope with an event of this scale. The disjoint between those with and those without has further exposed the complex differences in global health and social care systems in particular. Furthermore, the varying, often confused responses by many governments – caught under the influence of global pharmaceutical industries – to this global threat has been a notable feature of the pandemic. Public sector debilitation has added widespread challenges to already strained human development processes, complicating other ongoing global crises, including climate change, conflict (particularly in the Sahel, Ukraine and Yemen) and the global trafficking of people. Understanding the layering of this health crisis on top of others is important if the pandemic's impacts are to be mitigated and sustainable development achieved. When international development is taken into consideration, there is a need to repoint energies and resources towards those countries that are being most heavily affected through a lack of capacity or wealth. To bring this to the key issue, mitigation can only be half the answer – the future proofing that comes with development partnership is also critical for a genuine process of pandemic recovery.

The purpose of this book is to consider the pandemic's impacts across developmental scenarios, taking into account the timeline of the pandemic. In the first phase of the pandemic, the public health response was prioritized as the immediate challenge. In subsequent phases, economic effects and interactions with public health awareness, resource distribution and the shoring up of healthcare systems assumed greater prominence. What has been notable is that the respective phases required informed and targeted interventions resulting in changes to governance, public and social policy, locally and globally, and shifts in the culture of public responsibility. What became evident was the evolving form of political action, from border closures and restrictions on the freedom of movement (all with human rights implications) to national lockdowns. These difficulties were matched with economic stasis, job losses and shortages of healthcare equipment. In the medium term, in some cases, new institutional and social innovations – such as the heroic role of women's organizations and healthcare volunteers – emerged to cope with the contingencies of the public health crisis, dealing repeatedly with the mutation of the virus, different waves and geographic spread. In other cases, the virus was used to populist or political ends, or as a geopolitical weapon, with negative public health effects. In the longer term, two years after the initial outbreak, the situation became more precarious across much of the Global South, with health protectionism marking the roll out of strategic planning in the Global North. Indeed, policymakers in many places opted for national or regional responses – or disengagement – from global institutions and guidelines, such as those of the World Health Organization (WHO). Indeed, the United States' withdrawal from the WHO early in the pandemic gave legitimacy to other governments questioning the science. After two years, the initial WHO-driven consensus has for many states become superfluous to political motives and imperatives.

As a remit, this collection of chapters examines how the pandemic has been affecting different parts of the Global South through the outlook of international development. It looks at the formation of various government strategies at national and regional levels and assesses how effective they have been. It has brought together some of the most knowledgeable specialists in the field of development studies and furthers the conversation among those working in academia and nongovernmental organizations on addressing crisis situations pertinent to the pandemic. This dialogue on the subject aims to inform public debate, provide concise – mostly *in-situ* – insight and anticipates next steps. It attempts to suggest answers through critical engagement and is intended to be of use to development practitioners, policymakers, academics and those working to address the myriad issues the pandemic has created. It reflects on key problems that have arisen globally going into a third year of a pandemic and explores the implications for development planning. The emerging and reinforced disparities and disparate responses have caused the pandemic to affect regions and societies in radically different ways. This has also brought forward lessons. Indeed, what has emerged has been a cascade of crises: of solidarity, a global health provision meltdown and resulting socioeconomic inequalities – accentuating uneven development – that it will arguably take a generation from which to recover. Contributors focus on the development implications of this period, medical impacts, gender (in) equality, human rights derogations, regional disparities and the effects on marginal groups, vaccine monopolies and economic scarring, among other issues. Particular attention is paid to the increased risks faced by vulnerable populations, the diverging impact of policy interventions and often erratic governmental adaptation to the exigencies of public protection.

This book aims to contribute to social science and humanities research by investigating key issues and emerging concerns pertinent to the Global South in particular. It is a collaboration between the network and academic community grouped around the Development Studies Association Ireland, its partners around the world and with the support of Irish Aid. It is transdisciplinary and draws on perspectives from health, economics, geography, development practice, political science and other academic specialisms on themes relevant to international development, public and social policy. The scale of the pandemic and the socioeconomic shock across the

Global South needs to be looked at through a different lens to give those acting in the field a better critical knowledge base to help mitigate the effects of a protracted pandemic, particularly in highly vulnerable regions. The book's central objective is to generate discourse from a Development Studies' perspective on ways in which the impact of COVID-19 can be mitigated through development and where recovery can be envisaged in an integrated, equitable and sustainable manner.

PART I

Perspectives and Theory

ONE

Surviving Necropolitical Developments amid Democratic Disinformation: A Pandemic Perspective from Brazil

Su-ming Khoo and Mayara Floss

The global COVID-19 pandemic poses evolving dilemmas of disease, death, disability and economic and sociopolitical inequalities and injustices, as the SARS-CoV-2 virus continues to spread and variants evolve. This chapter reflects on the way disinformation has been used by reactionary and populist political actors in Brazil, with serious implications for the national health system (Sistema Único de Saúde, SUS) and global public health. Official misinformation and disinformation – promoting unproven 'early treatment', for example – impacts public understanding and health behaviours in a pandemic, negatively affecting public health systems and personnel as well as their capacities to prevent and minimize harm while deepening harmful, unequal and disequalizing effects. We argue that development and global health ethics warrant urgent and direct attention to *survival* in a context of a burning public sphere. Disinformation and necropolitics (the use of power to dictate how some people may live and some die) should be countered using a universal, rights-based approach to public health that gives equal attention to the public, democratic and scientific health bases of public health.

The ongoing global COVID-19 pandemic threatens the global population with illness, death and disability while also placing a magnifying glass or X-Ray on existing problems for democracies in every part of the world – including the largest in the Global South: India and Brazil (Heller, 2020). This contribution reflects on the challenges posed by disinformation in the broader context of reactionary, right-wing nationalist populism and mediatized political communications in Brazil. Sudden ('fast') crises like the pandemic have roots in, and connections to, 'slower', connected crises in which authoritarian, extractivist, necropolitical and even genocidal forms of 'development' are ongoing, deepening existing social divides, environmental and biological threats and vulnerabilities. This entanglement of problems leads some to define the COVID-19 crisis as a 'syndemic' (Horton, 2020) or 'omnicrisis' (Yong, 2021). Many people's lives, health and prospects are at stake, highlighting how 'crisis epistemology' must be countered by 'epistemologies of coordination' to prevent existing harms and inequalities from catastrophically worsening the situations of the already vulnerable and worst-off (Kara and Khoo, 2021; Whyte, 2021).

The threat of COVID-19 has led to increased investments to help overburdened health systems. However, health misinformation and disinformation are prevalent, salient and accelerated by social media. Inaccurate information seems to spread more quickly than scientifically reliable information, while many observe a general context of fear, anxiety and mistrust in institutions, science and experts (Wang et al, 2019; McKee et al, 2021). Misinformation and disinformation have serious implications for SUS and global public health, impacting the political, social and commercial determinants of health. They reflect, and contribute to, the deterioration of the democratic public sphere. Public authorities are finally being held to account at the highest level, as Brazil's president,

Jair Bolsonaro, and his government are charged with 'reckless handling of the pandemic', resulting in over 600,000 deaths from COVID-19 – including a disproportionate number of indigenous citizens – in the period up to November 2021. A Congressional inquiry suggests that government failures merit charges of 'crimes against humanity' (Philips, 2021).

This discussion considers problems of disinformation and misinformation, considering the publicness component as well as the scientific health component of public health. Health disinformation and misinformation have become part and parcel of a form of government-led, reactionary politics that corrode the ethos of public health universalism as embodied in the SUS system. 'Reactionary populism' is defined as a combination of antiliberal identity politics and liberal economic policies. It is associated with racist and exclusionary forms of nationalism and political sentiments mobilizing perceived losses of privilege and nostalgia for past privileges (González-Ruibal et al, 2018) in ways that are likely to harm less powerful groups and individuals.

Reactionary populism is rising in the context of epistemic crisis, a 'perfect neoliberal storm', in which information and the public sphere experience the confusion of post-truth politics (Cesarino, 2020). Post-truth is defined as 'relating to or denoting circumstances in which objective facts are less influential in shaping public opinion than appeals to emotion and personal belief' (OED, 'Post-truth'). The public may actually have the capacity to assess scientific reasoning and facts, but sections of it choose 'cultural cognition' according to emotions, ideological preferences or cynical interests (Anderson, 2012; Mukhtar, 2021). Lack of truth, hypocrisy and manipulation have always existed, but they have arguably become more normalized and heightened by the growth of digital and social media. Our increased reliance on digital communications brought on by pandemic restrictions has accentuated these trends. Governments may try to give the appearance of truthfulness and authenticity (Cesarino, 2020) while failing to control misinformation or even engaging in large-scale disinformation.

Reactionary politics and the epistemic determinants of health

Newman (2019) describes the post-truth turn as a profound transformation in public culture. Truth loses its symbolic authority, and there is less political need for information to be factually accurate. Davies (2016) observes that 'big data', forecasting and mood auditing have replaced the need for factual agreement, with chilling effects on politics. Without trusted statements about reality to work with, how can democracies agree on the nature of shared problems and solutions? Davies argues that conspiracy theories and cynical reasoning prosper in such conditions. We can quantify people's engagement with bad theories and reasoning but have few means to persuade people to reject cynical, self-serving postures and choose more equitable, solidaristic and less harmful behaviours.

The difference between facts and opinions has become blurred in the era of 'post-normal science' (Funtowitz and Ravetz, 1993). There are potential benefits from more pluralistic, diverse and shared forms of knowledge creation between scientists and other political and social actors, but this opening-up also brings new dilemmas. Science's truth claims have been destabilized and, as beliefs that definitive scientific truth exists become shaky, so does the public ground of social and political communication. Democracy requires public speech to be supported by people collectively believing that some degree of truth exists, and people need to care that information is correct. Lewandowsky et al (2017: 353) ask us to consider a situation where the public has 'had enough of experts', finds knowledge 'elitist' and relies instead on an opinion market such as Twitter to determine 'whether a newly emergent strain of avian flu is really contagious to humans'.

Negative impacts are not limited to any specific piece of misinformation. Misinformation impacts 'the overall intellectual well-being of a society', since declining trust in science correlates with declining social capital, increasing inequality and increasing social polarization. For example, misinformation has driven a worldwide increase in vaccine refusal, leading to substantial expense (Lewandowsky et al, 2017: 355), while children, poor and less educated parents are least empowered to counter vaccine misinformation.

Misinformation not only operates at the level of facts; it also operates through strategies, such as 'Deny, Attack, Reverse Victim–Offender'. Applied to the public sphere, this strategy contributes to general communicative disorder when powerful perpetrators deny facts, attack victims' credibility and assume the position of victim themselves while portraying less powerful victims as oppressive perpetrators (Harsey and Freyd, 2020). The game of epistemic reversal, doubt and relativism cynically and instrumentally manipulates positioning to monopolize power and dominate, attacking the real victims and misleading others. Alternative narratives about truth and politics continue to circulate and find traction, despite untruthful and harmful effects (Anderson, 2012; Jasanoff and Simmet, 2017). What can be done? In the rest of this essay, we reflect on Brazilian realities and developments that cannot be prevented but must be survived at the individual and the public, collective levels. Public things cannot be left to deteriorate and further fall into disrepair. As Honig (2017) argues, the public needs public things such as a functioning public health system, factual information and reliable, equitable services. Public things face destruction by forms of necropolitics that allow some to die while others may live (Mbembe, 2019). Public health protection and trustworthy information need to be maintained for a survivable democracy to remain possible for all (Honig, 2017; Maclean et al, 2020; MacMullen, 2020).

Today, we see the emergence of new concepts such as the 'political determinants of health' (Dawes, 2020) and the 'commercial determinants of health' (Mialon, 2020). Might these also be conditioned by the state of knowledge and 'epistemic determinants of health'? This crisis of knowledge, science and truth might be considered an epistemic crisis, with long-term and immediate consequences for people's health and survival.

'Democratic' disinformation? Brazil's 'early treatment' response

Wardle (2019) distinguishes between disinformation, which is knowingly false, deliberately created and disseminated, and misinformation, which is involuntarily spread without an explicit intention to deceive. On 24 October 2021, President Bolsonaro announced in his weekly live political broadcast that the COVID-19 vaccine could be linked to acquired immunodeficiency syndrome (AIDS) (Menon and Saldaña, 2021), an example of disinformation.

At the beginning of the global pandemic in March 2020, a hypothesis emerged that hydroxychloroquine could be used to treat people infected with COVID-19 (Gould and Norris, 2021). On 20 May 2020, Brazil's Ministry of Health announced the Early Drug Treatment Protocol (Brasil, 2020). However, by June 2020, the RECOVERY trial (Randomized Evaluation of Covid-19 Therapy) concluded that hydroxychloroquine was ineffective against severe COVID-19, and by early July 2020 hydroxychloroquine was not found to be a beneficial medical treatment (Gould and Norris, 2021). However, the Brazilian government persisted with its 'early treatment' programme until January 2021, when the Ministry of Health's website and publications were still continuing to recommend 'early treatment' using hydroxychloroquine.[1] There is no scientific evidence to support the term 'early treatment' in general (hence we choose to use it in quotation marks). The Ministry of Health's continued advocacy for 'early treatment' could be seen as misinformation up until July 2020 and disinformation subsequent to that (Siqueira and Monteiro, 2020), since robust studies disproving its effectiveness were widely known by public health authorities by that time (Gould and Norris, 2021; see also Floss et al, 2021; Freelon and Hanbury, 2021).

Misinformation is serious in the Brazilian context because three out of ten Brazilians are considered 'functionally illiterate', meaning they have limited ability to read, interpret texts, identify irony and perform mathematical operations in everyday life situations (Fajardo, 2018). The World Health Organization (WHO) points to the growing 'infodemic' problem, where there is too much information, including false or misleading information, in digital and physical environments during a disease outbreak. Infodemics cause confusion and risk-taking behaviours that can harm health, lead to mistrust in health authorities and undermine the public health response. An infodemic can intensify or lengthen outbreaks when people are unsure about what to do to protect their and others' health. The expanded digital realm of social media and internet spreads both benign and harmful information (WHO, nd, 'Infodemic'). We suggest that the concrete problem is not an abstract infodemic, but the disinfodemic spread under authoritarian, necropolitical styles of politics that create and spread a huge 'viral load' of potentially deadly disinformation (Posetti and Bontcheva, 2020).

Pontalti Monari et al (2020) argue that the pushback against preventative social isolation measures and the promotion of medically ineffective forms of 'early treatment' were convergent narratives strategically deployed by the federal government under Bolsonaro's leadership to manage a scenario where vaccines were unavailable. By November 2021, almost 60 per cent of the population were fully vaccinated against COVID-19 (Globo, 2021). Given the reactionary populist preference for a liberalized economy, one way to avoid restricting economic activities was to support the claim that hydroxychloroquine was an effective 'early treatment' (Pontalti Monari et al, 2020). Brazil's promotion of medically ineffective 'early treatment' has also been discussed as 'medical populism' (Casarões and Magalhães, 2021), a performative political style that responds to public health crises by misleadingly dividing 'the people' against 'the system', in this case their own public health system (Lasco, 2020). In the case of 'early treatment', its promotion by the government put doctors who remained unconvinced about its effectiveness and concerned about potential harm in a difficult position if they refused to dispense the treatment.

The Brazilian government's promotion and continuation of 'early treatment' may have provided the public with a false sense of security and weakened the enforcement of preventative and social isolation measures (Caponi et al, 2021). The population were also advised to attend health facilities at the first signs of disease, contributing to the rapid spread of the virus and increasing pressure on the SUS. The promotion of 'early treatment' risked overmedicalization – unnecessary medical intervention that does more harm than good – drug overuse and failure of quaternary prevention, the prevention of unethical and harmful overmedicalization (Depallens et al, 2020). Bolsonaro's pandemic strategy has followed a similar path to other right-wing authoritarian leaders (Rinaldi and Bekker, 2021) such as Rodrigo Duterte in the Philippines and Donald Trump in the United States: simplification, dramatization of responses, dismissing the media, questioning science and exploiting social divisions between the people and scapegoating and stigmatizing 'others' (Lasco, 2020). Medical populism gives the appearance of a legitimate debate, using rhetorical arguments, false scientific claims and denialism (Diethelm and McKee, 2009; Capelos et al, 2020: 186–90).

In 2020, national pharmaceutical companies received R$500 million from sales of 'early treatment' medication. Disinformation and misinformation linked to specific drugs (Melo et al, 2021) point to the significant costs of health commodification. The SUS ethos is to decommodify healthcare, providing cost-effective and medically effective healthcare as a public policy, thereby guaranteeing universal access to healthcare as a right. Decommodified, universal health systems are an equitable alternative to 'necropolitics', the politics of making profits live at the cost of some people's ill-health and death (Mbembe, 2019).

Necropolitics or survival? Disappearance in the flames

Disinformation and misinformation depend on affective, psychological responses and social contexts, and hence any attempt to counter them must involve a wider, interdisciplinary and collaborative effort (Wang et al, 2019) to understand the complex epistemic and ideological obstacles to effective health systems. Critical thinking and better health and media literacy are needed to help individuals and communities critically assess the credibility of information. But at the system level, the sharing of medically reliable and ethical information, and a systemic rejection of cynical necropolitics, needs to be cultivated, not least by the public institutions and professionals comprising the public health system.

Beyond the grievous and excessive number of deaths due to COVID-19, the very imagination, memory and ecological body of a shared country is going up in flames. In 2013, the Latin America Memorial burned down. In 2015, the Portuguese Language Museum was burnt. In 2018, the National Museum was destroyed by fire, and in 2021 the Cinemateca – housing the cinematographic imagination and memory of Brazil – also burned (Araujo, 2021). Among the reasons for these catastrophic fires was the lack of investment in fire plans for these major public institutions. Brazil and the Amazon's characteristic ecological biomes, the Cerrado and Pantanal, are also at risk of savannization and fire. The National Council for Scientific and Technological Development (Escobar, 2021) informed researchers in July 2021 that the server hosting the database of Brazilian researchers and the records of their research had been destroyed, containing the database and databank of Brazilian researchers. The future of scientific knowledge is also 'burning' from successive cuts to education and research, with thousands of university researchers in danger of losing their funding. Brazil's Bolsa Familia social protection programme – welfare support for a major proportion of the low-income population – has been repackaged by Bolsonaro's government as a new Auxilio Brasil programme, but many of its programmatic cornerstones have been cut or removed (Audi, 2021).

Amid the necropolitics of disinformation, failure to implement and adhere to pandemic control measures that actually work, and a policy of allowing the sick and infected to die, the main thing a health professional and public health scholar can do is to continue to fight for the survival of the public health system, and the public sphere, but also one's own survival as a human being. The pandemic demonstrates the indispensability of Brazil's hard-won public health system, SUS, and the importance of the right to health, despite a government that disinforms, negates and obstructs. SUS guarantees primary care, staffs the COVID-19 frontline, provides hospital care and, more recently, a vaccination programme. Amid the still-smouldering piles of ashes, the memory and public imagination of a shared country cannot be allowed to be forgotten and disappear. As the indigenous Brazilian leader Ailton Krenak (2020) said, 'we need ideas to postpone the end of the world'. The right to health and the unified health system are not only urgently needed to preserve lives and prevent deaths; they are ideas to postpone the end of the world and to build it back better, out of the ashes of so many fires.

Note

[1] The website can be consulted at https://www.gov.br/saude/pt-br

References

Anderson, E. (2012) 'Democracy, public policy, and lay assessments of scientific testimony', *Episteme*, 8(2): 144–64.

Araujo, I. (2021) 'Opinião: fogo na Cinemateca é uma política do governo com estudado descuido', *Folha de S.Paulo*. Available from: https://www1.folha.uol.com.br/ilustrada/2021/07/fogo-na-cinemateca-e-uma-politica-do-governo-com-estudado-descuido.shtml

Audi, A. (2021) 'Understanding Bolsonaro's new cash-transfer program', *Brazilian Report*, 1 November 2021. Available from: https://brazilian.report/society/2021/11/01/aid-bolsonaro-auxilio-brasil

Brasil (2020) *Orientações do ministério da saúde para manuseio medicamentoso precoce de pacientes com diagnóstico da COVID-19*, Brasília: Ministério da Saúde.

Capelos. T., Chrona, S., Salmela, M. and Bee, C. (2020) 'Reactionary politics and resentful affect in populist times', *Politics and Governance*, 9(3): 186–90.

Caponi, S., Brzozowski, F.S., Hellmann, F. and Bittencourt, S.C. (2021) 'O uso político da cloroquina: COVID-19, negacionismo e neoliberalismo / The political use of chloroquine: COVID-19, denialism and neoliberalism', *Revista Brasileira de Sociologia – RBS*, 9(21): 78–102.

Casarões, G. and Magalhães, D. (2021) 'The hydroxychloroquine alliance: how far-right leaders and alt-science preachers came together to promote a miracle drug', *Revista de Administração Pública*, 55(1): 197–214.

Cesarino, L. (2020) 'What the Brazilian 2018 elections tell us about post-truth in the neoliberal-digital era', *Cultural Anthropology*, 28 January 2020. Available from: https://culanth.org/fieldsights/what-the-brazilian-2018-elections-tell-us-about-post-truth-in-the-neoliberal-digital-era

Davies, W. (2016) 'The age of post-truth politics', *The New York Times*, 24 August 2016.

Dawes, D.E. (2020) *The Political Determinants of Health*, Baltimore: Johns Hopkins University Press.

Depallens, M.A., Guimarães, J.M.M. and Almeida Filho, N. (2020) 'Quaternary prevention: a concept relevant to public health?', *Cad Saude Publica*, 36(7). Available from: https://www.scielo.br/j/csp/a/qChZDxs9GVmJYd9PxC4YFwj/?lang=en.

Diethelm, P. and McKee, M. (2009) 'Denialism: what is it and how should scientists respond?', *European Journal of Public Health*, 19(1): 2–4.

Escobar, H. (2021) 'Orçamento 2021 compromete o futuro da ciência brasileira', *Jornal da USP*, 9 April. Available from: https://jornal.usp.br/ciencias/orcamento-2021-compromete-o-futuro-da-ciencia-brasileira

Fajardo, V. (2018) 'Como o analfabetismo funcional influencia a relação com as redes sociais no Brasil', *BBC News Brasil*, 11 December 2018. Available from: https://www.bbc.com/portuguese/brasil-46177957

Floss, M., Souza de Camargo, T., Tolotti, G. and Saldiva, P. (2021) *Cronologia do 'tratamento precoce' para COVID-19 no Brasil: desinformação e comunicação do Ministério da Saúde*. Available from: https://mediarxiv.org/kgm65/

Freelon, K. and Hanbury, S. (2021) 'Brazil's main COVID strategy is a cocktail of unproven drugs', *Undark*, 15 June.

Funtowitz, S. and Ravetz, J. (1993) 'Science for the post-normal age', *Futures*, 25(7): 739–55.

Globo (2021) 'Mapa da vacinação contra Covid-19 no Brasil'. Available from: https://especiais.g1.globo.com/bemestar/vacina/2021/mapa-brasil-vacina-covid

González-Ruibal, A., González, P.A. and Criado-Boado, F. (2018) 'Against reactionary populism: towards a new public archaeology', *Antiquity*, 92(362): 507–15.

Gould, S. and Norris, S.L. (2021) 'Contested effects and chaotic policies: the 2020 story of (hydroxy) chloroquine for treating COVID-19', *Cochrane Database of Systematic Reviews*, 3. Available from: https://cidg.cochrane.org/news/story-hydroxychloroquine-and-covid-19-new-cochrane-editorial

Harsey, S. and Freyd, J.J. (2020) 'Deny, attack, and reverse victim and offender (DARVO): what is the influence on perceived perpetrator and victim credibility?', *Journal of Aggression, Maltreatment & Trauma*, 29(8): 897–916.

Heller, P. (2020) 'The age of reaction: retrenchment populism in India and Brazil', *International Sociology*. Available from: https://journals.sagepub.com/doi/10.1177/0268580920949979

Honig, B. (2017) *Public Things: Democracy in Disrepair*, New York: Fordham University Press.

Horton, R. (2020) 'Offline: COVID-19 is not a pandemic', *Lancet*, 396(10255): 874.

Jasanoff, S. and Simmet, H.R. (2017) 'No funeral bells', *Social Studies of Science*, 47(5): 751–70.

Kara, H. and Khoo, S. (eds) (2021) *Qualitative and Digital Research in Times of Crisis*, Bristol: Bristol University Press.

Krenak, A. (2020) *Ideas to Postpone the End of the World*, Toronto: House of Anansi Press.

Laclau, E. (2005) *On Populist Reason*, London: Verso Books.

Lasco, G. (2020) 'Medical populism and the COVID-19 pandemic', *Global Public Health*, 15(10): 1417–29.

Lewandowsky, S., Ecker, U. and Cook, J. (2017) 'Beyond misinformation: coping with the post-truth era', *Journal of Applied Research in Memory and Cognition*, 6(4): 353–69.

Maclean, N., Imlay, A. and Wentz, M. (2020) 'Reactionary populism and the historical erosion of democracy in America: an interview with Nancy MacLean', *disClosure: A Journal of Social Theory*, 29 (July). Available from: https://uknowledge.uky.edu/disclosure/vol29/iss1/13

MacMullen, I. (2020) 'Survey article: what is postfactual politics?', *Journal of Political Philosophy*, 28(1): 97–116.

Mbembe, A. (2019) *Necropolitics*, Durham: Duke University Press.

McKee, M., Gugushvili, A., Koltai, J. and Stuckler, D. (2021) 'Are populist leaders creating the conditions for the spread of COVID-19?', *International Journal of Health Policy Management*, 10(8): 511–15.

Menon, I. and Saldaña, P. (2021) 'Bolsonaro faz associação absurda e falsa entre Aids e vacina de Covid, dizem especialistas', *Folha de S.Paulo*. Available from: https://www1.folha.uol.com.br/equil ibrioesaude/2021/10/bolsonaro-faz-associacao-absurda-e-falsa-entre-aids-e-vacina-de-covid-dizem-especialistas.shtml

Melo, J.R.R., Duarte, E.C., Vogler de Moraes, M., Fleck, K. and Dourado Arrais, P.S. (2021) 'Automedicação e uso indiscriminado de medicamentos durante a pandemia da COVID-19', *Cadernos de Saúde Pública*, 37: e00053221.

Mialon, M. (2020) 'An overview of the commercial determinants of health', *Global Health*, 16(74). Available from: https://link.sprin ger.com/article/10.1186/s12992-020-00607-x

Mukhtar, A. (2021) 'Psychology and politics of COVID-19 misinfodemics: why and how do people believe in misinfodemics?', *International Sociology*, 36(1): 111–23.

Newman, S. (2019). 'Post-truth and the crisis of the political', *Soft Power*, 6(2): 91–108.

Pontalti Monari, A.C., Santos, A. and Sacramento, I. (2020) 'COVID-19 and (hydroxy)chloroquine: a dispute over scientific truth during Bolsonaro's weekly Facebook live streams', *Journal of Science Communication*, 19(7): A03.

Posetti, J. and Bontcheva, K. (2020) *Disinfodemic: Dissecting Responses to COVID-19 Disinformation* (2nd edn), Paris: UNESCO.

Rinaldi, C. and Bekker, M.P.M. (2021) 'A scoping review of populist radical right parties' influence on welfare policy and its implications for population health in Europe', *International Journal of Health Policy Management*, 10(3): 141–51.

Siqueira, F.C. and de Monteiro, P. (2020) 'Jornalismo em tempos de pandemia', João Pessoa: Universidade Federal da Paraíba. Available from: http://www.ccta.ufpb.br/ppj/contents/livros/jornalismo-em-tempos-de-pandemia.pdf

Wang, Y., McKee, M., Torbica, A. and Stuckler, D. (2019) 'Systematic literature review on the spread of health-related misinformation on social media', *Social Science and Medicine*, 240: 112552.

Wardle, C. (2019) 'Information disorder: the techniques we saw in 2016 have evolved', *First Draft News*. Available from: https://fir stdraftnews.org/articles/information-disorder-the-techniques-we-saw-in-2016-have-evolved

Whyte, K. (2021) 'Against crisis epistemology', in B. Hokowhitu, A. Moreton-Robinson, L. Tuhiwai-Smith, S. Larkin and C. Andersen (eds), *Handbook of Critical Indigenous Studies*, London: Routledge.

WHO (nd) 'Infodemic'. Available from: https://www.who.int/hea lth-topics/infodemic#tab=tab_1

Yong, E. (2021) 'What even counts as science writing anymore?', *The Atlantic*, 2 October 2021. Available from: https://www.thea tlantic.com/science/archive/2021/10/how-pandemic-changed-science-writing/620271

TWO

COVID-19, International Development and the Global Economy

Stephen McCloskey and Amit Prakash

Since the 1980s, international development and the global economy have been aligned with neoliberalism, the free market ideology first implemented to disastrous effect in Chile in the 1970s (Doane, 2011). The neoliberal playbook for development in the Global South was formulated in prescriptive, 'one size fits all', market-oriented reforms known as the Washington Consensus (Gore, 2000). The Washington Consensus prescribed low taxes, free trade, self-regulation rather than state-regulation, the privatization of public services and the free movement of capital (Mason, 2021: 51). Neoliberalism represented a major swing from the state-led development that dominated economic relations in the post-Second World War period under the influence of Keynesianism to market-led development in the 1970s onwards under the influence of neoliberal economist Milton Friedman. The outcomes of neoliberalism included a highly unequal distribution of wealth heavily skewed towards the wealthiest 1 per cent. Oxfam found that 'between 1988 and 2011, 46 per cent of overall income growth accrued to the top 10 per cent, while the bottom 10 per cent received only 0.6 percent' (2016: 9). While the size of the global economy doubled in the 30 years from 1985 to 2015, the wealthiest 1 per cent received a higher percentage of global income growth than the entire bottom 50 per cent combined (2016: 9). By 2021, it was Oxfam's assessment that 'for 40 years, the richest 1 per cent have earned more than double the income of the bottom half of the global population' (Oxfam, 2021: 9).

These inequalities preceded two shuddering jolts that shook the global economy to its core: the 2008 global financial crisis and the 2020 pandemic. Both events have exposed the flawed and chaotic nature of the neoliberal economic system, with the idea that the market was self-regulating and best untethered from the stewardship of the state now discredited (Tooze, 2021). This chapter examines the pandemic's impact on the global economy and international development. By way of an example, the second half of the chapter considers the case of India, where privatized services, particularly healthcare, were overwhelmed by the challenges of COVID-19 following decades of neoliberal reform.

The inequality virus

By the end of the Cold War, the buoyancy of the free market and the ideological triumph of liberal globalization over state capitalism in the former Soviet Union and its satellites prompted American political scientist, Francis Fukuyama, to declare the 'end of history', arguing that Western liberal democracy 'could not be improved on' and represented the endpoint of ideological evolution (Fukuyama, 1992: xi). The drive for deregulation under neoliberalism, however, removed restraints from the banking sector to separate savings and investment divisions and resulted in speculative lending, mostly in the property market. When Lehman Brothers collapsed in 2008, the global banking sector was sitting on a pile of toxic debt that needed a state rescue package not seen since the Great Depression to prevent the banks from going under

(Grice, 2009; Collins, 2015). The response to the crisis in the European Union and North America was to double-down on neoliberalism by imposing wage freezes, cutting public services and eroding the welfare state, an austerity programme imposed under the guise of debt management. The results were predictably disastrous. By the end of the decade following the crash, 3.4 billion people were living on less than $5.50 per day, with the rate of poverty reduction having halved since 2013 from 1 per cent a year to 0.5 per cent a year. In the same period, the number of billionaires doubled (Oxfam, 2019: 9–10).

The COVID-19 pandemic, therefore, impacted on the global economy at a time of extreme vulnerability for millions across the world already struggling to meet essential needs after ten years of austerity. Described as the 'inequality virus' by Oxfam, COVID-19 has 'exposed, fed off and increased existing inequalities of wealth, gender and race' (Oxfam, 2021: 2). Former United Nations' Rapporteur on Extreme Poverty and Human Rights, Philip Alston, similarly suggested that 'COVID-19 is a pandemic of poverty, exposing the parlous state of social safety nets for those on lower incomes or in poverty around the world' (2020: 9). As in 2008, it was the taxpayer who came to the rescue, with central banks injecting $9 trillion into economies worldwide. Once again, billionaires benefitted, with much of that stimulus going into financial markets and 'from there into the net worth of the ultra-rich' (Sharma, 2021). India, for example, saw the wealth of billionaires soar to more than 17 per cent of its gross domestic product (GDP), one of the highest shares in the world. Globally, Forbes' annual rich list in 2021 recorded the number of billionaires at 2,755, an increase of 660 on 2020 (Forbes, 2021). The collective fortune of these billionaires was £13.1 trillion, an increase of $8 trillion on 2020, pointing to how the super-rich had profited from the stock-market, with the world's richest person, Jeff Bezos, earning $13bn in just one day (20 July 2020) at the height of the pandemic (Neate, 2020). A few months earlier, in April 2020, 20 million

Americans were reported unemployed, the highest jobless total (at 14.7 per cent) since the Great Depression, as shuttered businesses shed workers during extended economic lockdowns (Kelly, 2020).

While the state response to the 2008 crisis was to squeeze wages and force us to work harder for less, the pandemic demanded that economic activity be severely contracted and that most employees stay at home. The world also discovered just how 'essential' public-facing, frontline workers were to our surviving COVID-19. They included drivers, bin-men and women, supermarket workers, carers and of course health workers. By July 2020, a few months into the pandemic, Amnesty International (2020) calculated that 3,000 health workers in 79 countries had died after contracting COVID-19. Moreover, 60 per cent of the 540 health workers who died in the UK identified as being members of the Black and minority ethnic sector (Amnesty International, 2020). The pandemic preyed upon and exposed the sexism and racism inherent in the neoliberal economic system. Oxfam reported in early 2021 that in Brazil, people of Afro-descent were 40 per cent more likely to die of COVID-19 than White people. By June 2020, 9,200 Afro-descendants would still have been alive if their death rate had been the same as White people (Oxfam, 2021: 8). Oxfam summarized how neoliberalism had underpinned and entrenched the inequalities exposed by COVID-19 when it suggested: 'This inequality is the product of a flawed and exploitative economic system, which has its roots in neoliberal economics and the capture of politics by elites. It has exploited and exacerbated entrenched systems of inequality and oppression, namely patriarchy and structural racism, ingrained in white supremacy' (Oxfam, 2021: 10).

Neoliberal retreat?

Some economists (MacFarlane, 2021; Mason, 2021) have sourced the pandemic itself to the economic system's encroachment on nature, which has transmitted animal diseases to humans. COVID-19 is 'not a random act of God', argues MacFarlane: 'Like climate change, it is a symptom of accelerating environmental breakdown, which in turn is a product of an economic model that is reliant on growth and accumulation' (MacFarlane, 2021: 123). Government responses to the pandemic ripped up the austerity narrative of the post-2008 period by injecting massive amounts of spending into fiscal supports to businesses and the furloughing of workers. The International Monetary Fund estimated the total global spend at $9 trillion by May 2020, which suggested that the days of 'slash and burn' economics were over (Battersby et al, 2020). While much of this fiscal support delivered corporate welfare to undeserving multinationals (Reich, 2020), governments appeared to concede that the austerity approach of low taxes, a small state and balanced budgets had to be abandoned to rescue the global economy. The state appears to be back as a development actor after COVID-19 exposed the collective jeopardy arising from the chronic underfunding of public services, particularly healthcare (Lal et al, 2020). In India (our example), the government has stubbornly implemented neoliberalism despite the chronic problems that have beset the health sector and wider economy during the pandemic. These problems are considered in the next section.

Entrenched neoliberalism amid emerging neo-Keynesianism

The root causes of the social misery that was reported during the COVID-19 pandemic are embedded deep in the structure of neoliberalism. The pandemic set forth in sharp relief the negative impacts of the unbridled pursuit of profit, while – in many regions – whittling away the hard-fought social welfare infrastructure. The reasons for the incapacity of the public systems to respond adequately to the heath emergency were not episodic, nor will such incapacities disappear with the pandemic. Both the causes and the impact are a function of four decades of conscious policy shifts towards a set of neoliberal prescriptions – including in the health sector.

The eruption of large-scale infection during the COVID-19 pandemic in the first quarter of 2020 was a cataclysmic event for many across the world. While the large-scale illness and death was indeed a shock, what was even more unbelievable was the swiftness with which public health systems came under severe strain due to the pressure of citizens seeking curative assistance. Even though a series of platitudes were expressed about the health infrastructure being overwhelmed, the reasons for such an outcome are not difficult to find under neoliberal policy prescriptions, which have hollowed out the liberal state and led to a concomitant shrinkage of public services (Rao, 2010). The simplest way to underline this argument is to look at the sources of health expenditure in India between 2000 and 2018 (WHO, nd). Public expenditure on health remained low throughout the previous two decades, with some spikes but registering a sharp decline in more recent years. Further, over the past two decades, out-of-pocket spending on health – money spent from regular earnings without any public or insurance support – makes up around three quarters of the total expenditure on health. It should thus be no surprise that the health system faced a veritable collapse under the demands of treatment during the pandemic. In different terms, the right of – or to – life itself was thus forced into a contested reality owing to the decline in the public health infrastructure (Singh et al, 2020: 1).

Excess deaths in India owing to the incapacity of the health system is a fact, the precise scale of which is a subject of debate. While official data claimed around 461,000 deaths as of 7 November 2021, some experts have calculated this figure to be underreported by a factor of 5 or more (Hindu Data Team, 2021). The scale of death owing to the pandemic was such that in the absence of financial wherewithal, thousands could not be cremated and were consigned to rivers or buried in shallow graves along the river beds (Pandey, 2021). Further, the overwhelming of the hollowed out public health system was also evident in the acute shortage of medical oxygen and other treatments at the peak of the pandemic – something that needed an order by the Supreme Court to be addressed (Supreme Court Suo Motu Writ Petition [Civil] no[s]. 6/2020). Such orders from the apex court notwithstanding, the degree to which the issue could be addressed by the under-capacitated state and the overwhelmed health system is questionable.

Another slice in the story of the neoliberal state that added to the misery and pain of the pandemic was the delay in rolling out the vaccine owing to the depletion of the country's vaccine capacity (Bhushan, 2021). Privatization of large public sector vaccine manufacturing capacity under the neoliberal reforms ensured that the country was dependent on one corporate manufacturer – the Serum Institute of India, which in turn needed time to ramp up production to the scale required. Further, even amid the devastation of the pandemic, the state was unwilling to commit resources to enhance production capacity: no public support was extended for the development of a vaccine or expansion of production facilities until the advance order was placed as late as January 2021 (Anand, 2021). The state was careful not to tread on corporate toes, the Supreme Court's nudge towards compulsory licensing notwithstanding. The Indian public ultimately paid one of the highest rates for vaccination by the private sector. While public health institutions offer free vaccination, the depletion of such institutions meant delayed delivery, which it was vital to avoid if the pandemic was to be managed effectively. An additional factor also needs to be underlined. The neoliberal reforms in healthcare had lionized the private health providers as a solution to the gaps resulting from the depleted public infrastructure. The experience of the pandemic highlighted the extremely limited capacity of private health providers, which were easily and quickly overwhelmed by the sheer numbers involved. Furthermore, even the small proportion of people that could afford their services were left to shuttle around, losing lives waiting for a bed to become available in five-star private hospitals.

The social costs of a hollowed out Indian state owing to neoliberal reforms also unfolded in what has come to be known as the great migrant workers' crisis of 2020 (Infante, 2020). The challenge to the right to life itself was clearly visible in the incapacity and unwillingness of the state to step up and take responsibility for supplying food to migrant workers stranded owing to the sudden imposition of a stringent lockdown from 24 March 2020 (Government of India, 2020a). The workers were suddenly left without work and access to wages and, therefore, food. Such incapacity of the state, due to a misplaced concern with public finances, meant that millions of migrant workers had no recourse but to literally walk home to their villages. Many died of sheer exhaustion, hunger, thirst or in accidents (Rawat, 2020). The government's chief law officer claimed in court that there were no workers on the country's highways, notwithstanding hundreds of media reports to the contrary (Prakash, 2021). The extremely meagre support that did materialize was captured in the Stranded Workers Action Network (SWAN) survey of April 2020, which found that '96 per cent [of those entitled] had not received rations from the government and 70 per cent had not received any cooked food' (SWAN, 2020a). In the following month, the story remained extremely bleak: 'About 82 per cent … had not received rations from the government and 68 per cent … had not received any cooked food' (SWAN, 2020b). No income support was extended, and the support to farmers and businesses that was extended was in the form of 'softer' loans and not budgetary support.

Ad hoc support that the state extended for employment to the poor was in the form of unskilled employment under the Mahatma Gandhi National Rural Employment Guarantee

Act (MGNREGA) 2005. This provides for a demand-driven 100 days' employment during the lean season. Work provided under the MGNREGA is manual unskilled earth work at the basic wage rate. This programme – which the current ruling Bhartiya Janata Party (Beg, 2020) had reviled as a 'living monument of [the] failure' of the earlier United Progressive Alliance government – saw a spurt in demand for work despite it being one that only provides unskilled manual work at very low wages. This demand emphasized the extremely distressed condition of workers – but even this avenue of eking out an extremely precarious living faltered since the number of jobs provided in April 2020 under MGNREGA was lower than that provided in the same month in 2019. Such precariousness of the right to livelihood under the neoliberal state was not limited to the poor, unskilled migrant workers between April and July 2020 – 18.9 per cent of salaried employees also lost their jobs (Vyas, 2020), with 6 million professional jobs lost. This erasure of the right to life and livelihood was compounded by GDP contracting by 23.9 per cent during the first quarter of 2020–21 – the first economic contraction in four decades (Anon, 2020). This state of employment and absent public support needs to be contrasted with the meteoric rise in the wealth of the rich and corporates during the pandemic.

The conundrum that arises from the Indian state's management of the pandemic is the following: in a world witnessing a flurry of neo-Keynesianism, the Indian state is among the few states that continue to soldier on with neoliberal policies. The grudging and meagre social relief that has been extracted from public funds as short-term relief is indeed just that: ad hoc, short-term relief. The desperate relief measures announced by the Finance Minister in a press conference on 14 May 2020 (Government of India, 2020b) were steeped in neoliberalism. The challenge thus remains to construct a global public policy consensus towards an expansion of an interventionist (neo-Keynesian) model, where publicly funded social rights become the cornerstone of any economic growth and where public services are not merely resources for financing the aggrandisement of the rich.

References

Alston, P. (2020) 'The parlous state of poverty eradication: report of the Special Rapporteur on Extreme Poverty and Human Rights', Human Rights Council, 2 July. Available from: https://chrgj.org/wp-content/uploads/2020/07/Alston-Poverty-Report-FINAL.pdf

Amnesty International (2020) 'UK among highest COVID-19 health worker deaths in the world', 13 July. Available from: https://www.amnesty.org.uk/press-releases/uk-among-highest-covid-19-health-worker-deaths-world

Anand, U. (2021) 'No funds granted for vaccine research, development: govt', *Hindustan Times* (New Delhi), 11 May. Available from: https://www.hindustantimes.com/india-news/no-funds-granted-for-vaccine-research-development-govt-101620675320843.html

Anon (2020) 'First economic contraction in 4 decades: India's GDP shrinks 23.9% in Q1, FY21', *Business Standard*, 31 August. Available from: https://www.business-standard.com/article/economy-policy/first-economic-contraction-in-4-decades-india-s-gdp-shrinks-x-in-q1-fy21-120083101022_1.html

Battersby, B., Raphael Lam, W. and Ture, E. (2020) 'Tracking the $9 trillion global fiscal support to fight COVID-19', IMF Blog, 20 May 2020. Available from: https://blogs.imf.org/2020/05/20/tracking-the-9-trillion-global-fiscal-support-to-fight-covid-19

Beg, M.A. (2020) 'Once called "living monument of UPA's failures" by PM Modi, will MGNREGA help during Covid-19?', *Outlook*, 18 May. Available from: https://www.outlookindia.com/website/story/news-analysis-once-called-living-monument-of-upas-failures-by-pm-modi-will-mgnrega-help-during-covid-19/353019

Bhushan, B. (2021) 'Who destroyed India's vaccine self-sufficiency?', *Business Standard*, 17 May. Available from: https://www.business-standard.com/article/opinion/who-destroyed-india-s-vaccine-self-sufficiency-121051700112_1.html

Collins, M. (2015) 'The big bank bailout', *Forbes Magazine*, 14 July. Available from: https://www.forbes.com/sites/mikecollins/2015/07/14/the-big-bank-bailout/#2e80a7b32d83

Doane, D. (2011) 'Neoliberal policies have no place in the post-crash world', *The Guardian*, 23 March. Available from: https://www.theguardian.com/global-development/poverty-matters/2011/mar/23/neoliberal-policies-discredited

Forbes (2021) 'World's billionaires list: the richest in 2021'. Available from: https://www.forbes.com/billionaires

Fukuyama, F. (1992) *The End of History and the Last Man*, London: Penguin.

Gore, C. (2000) 'The rise and fall of the Washington Consensus as a paradigm for developing countries', *World Development*, 28(5): 789–804.

Government of India (2020a) 'Ministry of Home Affairs order no. 40-3/2020-DM-I(A)', 24 March. Available from: https://www.mha.gov.in/sites/default/files/MHAorder%20copy_0.pdf

Government of India (2020b) 'PowerPoint slides of the finance minister's speech part-2: poor, including migrants and farmers 14.05.2020'. Available from: https://covid19.india.gov.in/document-category/ministry-of-finance

Grice, A. (2009) '850bn: the official cost of the bank bailout', *The Independent*, 4 December. Available from: https://www.independent.co.uk/news/uk/politics/163850bn-official-cost-of-the-bank-bailout-1833830.html

Hindu Data Team (2021) '"Excess deaths" during the pandemic in India was 5.8 times the official COVID-19 death toll', *The Hindu*, 11 September. Available from: https://bit.ly/3o1sDhk

Infante, S. (2020) 'India's coronavirus migration crisis', JStor Daily, 17 June. Available from: https://daily.jstor.org/indias-migration-crisis

Kelly, J. (2020) 'U.S. unemployment is at its highest rate since the Great Depression at 14.7% – with 20.5 million more jobs lost in April', *Forbes*. Available from: https://www.forbes.com/sites/jackkelly/2020/05/08/us-unemployment-is-at-its-highest-rate-since-the-great-depression-at-147-with-205-million-more-jobs-lost-in-april/?sh=3c986ce5656d

Lal, A., Erondu, N., Heymann, D., Gitahi, G. and Yates, R. (2020) 'Fragmented health systems in COVID-19: rectifying the misalignment between global health security and universal health coverage', *The Lancet*, 1 December, 61–7. Available from: https://www.thelancet.com/action/showPdf?pii=S0140-6736%2820%2932228-5

MacFarlane, L. (2021) 'Why 2021 is humanity's make or break moment on climate breakdown', *Policy and Practice: A Development Education Review*, 32(Spring): 120–9.

Mason, P. (2021) *How to Stop Fascism: History, Ideology, Resistance*, London: Allen Lane.

Neate, R. (2020) 'Jeff Bezos, the world's richest man, added £10bn to his fortune in just one day', *The Guardian*, 21 July.

Oxfam (2016) 'An economy for the 1%: how privilege and power in the economy drive extreme inequality and how this can be stopped', Oxford: Oxfam. Available from: https://www-cdn.oxfam.org/s3fs-public/file_attachments/bp210-economy-one-percent-tax-havens-180116-en_0.pdf

Oxfam (2019) 'Public good or private wealth?', Oxford: Oxfam. Available from: https://oxfamilibrary.openrepository.com/bitstream/handle/10546/620599/bp-public-good-or-private-wealth-210119-summ-en.pdf

Oxfam (2021) 'The inequality virus: bringing together a world torn apart by coronavirus through a fair, just and sustainable economy', Oxford: Oxfam. Available from: https://oxfamilibrary.openrepository.com/bitstream/handle/10546/621149/bp-the-inequality-virus-summ-250121-en.pdf

Pandey, G. (2021) 'Covid-19: India's holiest river is swollen with bodies', BBC News, 19 May. Available from: https://www.bbc.com/news/world-asia-india-57154564

Prakash, A. (2021) 'Shadow of the pandemic and the Beleaguered Liberal-Democratic script in India', *India Review*, 20(2): 104–20.

Rao, M. (2010) '"Health for all" and neoliberal globalisation: an Indian rope trick', *Socialist Register*, 46: Morbid Symptoms, 262–78.

Rawat, M. (2020) 'Migrant workers' deaths: govt says it has no data; but didn't people die? Here is a list', *India Today*, 16 September. Available from: https://www.indiatoday.in/news-analysis/story/migrant-workers-deaths-govt-says-it-has-no-data-but-didn-t-people-die-here-is-a-list-1722087-2020-09-16

Reich, R. (2020) 'Coronavirus exposes the height of corporate welfare', *Salon*, 23 April 2020. Available from: https://www.salon.com/2020/04/23/robert-reich-coronavirus-exposes-the-height-of-corporate-welfare_partner

Sharma, R. (2021) 'The billionaire boom: how the super-rich soaked up Covid cash'. *Financial Times*, 14 May. Available from: https://www.ft.com/content/747a76dd-f018-4d0d-a9f3-4069bf2f5a93

Singh, A., Deedwania, P., K. V., Chowdhury, A.R., Khanna, P. (2020) 'Is India's health care infrastructure sufficient for handling COVID 19 pandemic?', *International Archive of Public Health Community Medicine*, 4(2): 1–4. DOI: 10.23937/2643-4512/1710041

Supreme Court Suo Motu Writ Petition (Civil) no(s), 6/2020 in 'Re: problems and miseries of migrant labourers', SCC Online SC 490, SCC Online SC 492, and SCC Online SC 613.

SWAN (2020a) '21 days and counting: COVID-19 lockdown, migrant workers, and the inadequacy of welfare measures in India', SWAN. Available from: http://publications.azimpremjifoundation.org/2272/1/lockdown_and_distress_report_by_stranded_workers_action_network-2.pdf

SWAN (2020b) '32 days and counting: COVID-19 lockdown, migrant workers, and the inadequacy of welfare measures in India', SWAN. Available from: https://covid19socialsecurity.files.wordpress.com/2020/05/32-days-and-counting_swan.pdf?fbclid=IwAR0-kuFz9pV9drrshn7NLnOUOuVbkv7NbrGzcqMLBMwyel0isEsaoLO-dw0

Tooze, A. (2021) 'Has Covid ended the neoliberal era?', *The Guardian*, 2 September. Available from: https://www.theguardian.com/news/2021/sep/02/covid-and-the-crisis-of-neoliberalism

Vyas, M. (2020) 'An unhealthy recovery', CMIE. Available from: https://www.cmie.com/kommon/bin/sr.php?kall=warti cle&dt=2020-08-18%2011:02:19&msec=596

WHO (nd) 'Global health expenditure database'. Available from: https://apps.who.int/nha/database/country_profile/Index/en

THREE

Global Finance and the COVID-19 Pandemic in Africa

Howard Stein and Rick Rowden

In July 2021, Africa entered a third wave of COVID-19 after eight straight weeks of rising cases, hospitalization and deaths. In January 2022, Africa was hit by a fourth wave, after six continual weeks of surging numbers. Given the low vaccination rates and appearance of new variants, these waves are likely to re-occur for some time. Many writers have pointed to causes like vaccine apartheid and the grabbing of health supplies by wealthy countries, while others have focused on poverty and the lack of health goods and service capacities in African countries. Less has been written on how the historical patterns of financial flows and the nature of the global financial system have contributed to the conditions that exacerbate the impact of the pandemic.

Crises such as the current pandemic expose the gross inequities of our global economic order. African countries found themselves woefully unprepared for the pandemic, made worse by the hyper-nationalism in the West that has restricted the imports of key health goods – including pharmaceutical products. Even before the crisis, there was an absence of basic personal protective equipment, testing capacity, hospital and emergency room beds, ventilators and even medical oxygen, which was the single most important measure to prevent death for those severely ill. Treatments like monoclonal antibodies are almost non-existent in African countries. Though vaccines have proven highly effective against the virus, most African countries have had little or no access to them. Through the second week of April 2022, only 15.9 per cent of the continent's population had been fully vaccinated, with coverage very uneven. A few countries, like Mauritius and the Seychelles, have high vaccination rates exceeding 75 per cent of their population. A third of African countries have rates under 7 per cent.[1]

How is it that African countries, 60 years after independence, must still rely on the outside world for commodities that are central to the health and welfare of their populations? The answer partly lies in the nature of the global financial system. Over the past 40 of those years, there has been a massive explosion of financial flows, partly due to widespread capital account liberalization, which removed barriers to flows, growth of diaspora populations, growing concentration of wealth in search of returns globally and the expansion of the power of multinational corporations and their ability to move capital around in support of value chain-based production. The flows have not only included foreign direct investment (FDI) but also portfolio capital in the form of stocks and private and public bond issues, lending from private and state banks and other financial institutions, bilateral and multilateral aid, remittances and other types of transfers such as profit-shifting for purposes of tax avoidance. This chapter will investigate how these global financial flows have affected the structure of African economies in general and will assess, in particular, their capacities to deal with the COVID-19 pandemic.

Historical patterns of flows

The key characteristic of the global financial architecture is the hierarchy of currencies that has helped determine how countries interact with the global economy. Money has four basic functions: a store of value, a unit of account, a medium of exchange and a standard of deferred payment. The United States is at the top of the hierarchy due to its capacity to fulfil these functions well. The dollar is still overwhelmingly the main unit of account in international transactions, including the generation of international debt. At the bottom of the hierarchy are countries on the periphery, including those in Africa. There is little confidence among economic players in the global economy in the capacity of these countries' currencies to provide stability as a store of value or unit of account. This creates monetary and economic dependency, which constrains policy space, reduces sovereignty and shapes African countries' social, political and economic structures. Under this unequal global system, African and other developing countries must export goods to advanced economies or attract flows in order to get the hard currencies needed for crucial imports, to service external liabilities and deal with the rapid capital outflows that have become more challenging in the era of capital account liberalization.

These global financial inequities have contributed to the domination of the neoliberal development model, which has undermined African countries' capacities to develop their economies through structural transformation, that is, the transition over time from an economy based on primary agriculture and extractive industries towards one based more on manufacturing – which pays higher wages. Since the 1980s, foreign aid, policy advice and loan conditions from the International Monetary Fund (IMF), World Bank and Western-led bilateral aid agencies have compelled African countries to reduce the role of the state in supporting the development of domestic manufacturing and economic diversification. The result has been that many African economies remain stuck as low-end primary commodity producers with low wages, high unemployment and underemployment, and low domestic tax bases that are incapable of financing adequate health and education provision. This failure to promote development has left African economies particularly susceptible to global shocks such as the COVID-19 crisis. The failure of the neoliberal development model has also left African economies locked into export commodity dependence, where the price of agricultural and mineral exports has tended to be volatile, particularly in respect of manufactured goods (UNCTAD, 2019).

Negative commodity price shocks such as the economic fallout from the pandemic force governments into balance of payments crises, which frequently means turning to outside agencies like the IMF (UNCTAD, 2019; Loscher, 2022). The IMF provides emergency financial assistance to developing economies based on loan conditions that call for fiscal austerity (reductions in public spending), lowering wages and raising interest rates – all of which are designed to make the country import less and export more so that creditworthiness is re-established. However, many critics – including the IMF's own research department – have concluded that cutting public spending during an economic crisis can actually make the crisis deeper, longer, slow its recovery and cause damage to workforce productivity in contrast to outcomes if countries increased public spending (Ostry et al, 2016). While the IMF was quick to disburse billions in new emergency loans to developing countries in 2020 in response to the COVID crisis, most of these loan programmes called for fiscal austerity in 2021, 2022 and 2023, even as the economic fallout from COVID – now exacerbated by the war in Ukraine – is likely to continue (Ortiz and Cummins, 2021).

Consequently, many developing countries go to great lengths to avoid having to appeal to the IMF for emergency financial support during a crisis by increasing hard currency reserves. Augmenting foreign exchange reserves provides greater policy space to begin to address commodity dependence, but the pressing need for reserves pushes governments to maximize commodity exports and accumulate reserves during good times rather than spending down these reserves to diversify their economies away from commodity dependency. Hence, in the current financial order, African economies are stuck in a vicious cycle of commodity dependence.[2]

The impact of neoliberalism on the continent is well documented (Mhone, 1995; Stein and Nissanke, 1999; Mkandawire, 2001).[3] Briefly, neoliberal policy reforms under IMF and World Bank structural adjustment programmes entailed market liberalization, privatization, macro-stabilization and charging user fees in health and education, which were supposed to lead to gains in static efficiency but instead led to exclusion for the poorest. Social expenditure cuts and the privatization of social services in healthcare and education put African countries in worse health in the 1980s and 1990s and on the wrong trajectory to combat any future pandemic. Declines in spending in an already poorly developed infrastructure, low productivity and declining standards of living attracted little FDI in areas other than raw material extraction (Stein, 2013).

Neoliberal policy reforms included capital account liberalization, which reduced restrictions on capital flows, privatization or closure of state-owned enterprises and prematurely liberalizing trade, all of which undermined local manufacturing capacity and led to greater reliance on imports of manufacturing goods, including pharmaceuticals and other health commodities. The failure of the neoliberal model is reflected in Africa's increasing dependence on exporting unprocessed raw materials for foreign exchange. The United Nations Conference on Trade and Development (UNCTAD) defines a country as dependent on commodities when they account for more than 60 per cent of its total merchandise exports in value terms. Its State of Commodity Dependence Report 2019 finds that the number of commodity-dependent countries increased from 92 between 1998 and 2002 to 102 between 2013 and 2017, leaving more than half of the world's countries (102 out of 189) and two thirds of developing countries dependent on commodities. Sub-Saharan African (SSA) economies are the hardest-hit, with 89 per cent of the region's countries commodities-dependent.

The neoliberal model has led to the deindustrialization of the continent and returned Africa to its colonial-style extraction economy with its problematic boom and bust commodity cycles. For example, manufacturing fell from 17 per cent of GDP from 1979 to 1981 to only 10.7 per cent from 2000 to 2009 to 9.4 per cent from 2010 to 2019 (Stein, 2013; UNCTAD, 2021). Figure 3.1 contrasts manufacturing value added as a percentage of GDP for South Korea, which followed in the steps of the advanced economies by giving the state a strong role in building domestic manufacturing over time, and SSA economies, which followed the neoliberal model to undo state support for building manufacturing.

Figure 3.1: MVA (manufacturing value added) as a percentage of GDP for South Korea and Sub-Saharan Africa, 1960–2020

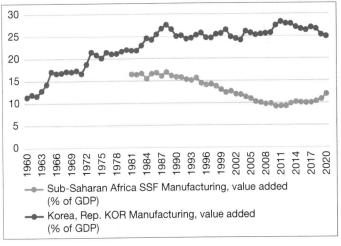

Source: World Bank databank. See https://data.worldbank.org/indicator/NV.IND.MANF.ZS?locations=KR-ZG

Table 3.1 provides details on the comparative importance of three types of key financial inflows into Africa that are vitally important for Africa to sustain itself in the global financial order: official development assistance – foreign aid (ODA), remittances and FDI. The figure for 1990 was indicative of the numbers over the 1990s during the adjustment period. Remittances and FDI were tiny relative to ODA. African countries had little or no access to private finance in the 1980s and 1990s. Between 1980 and 1998, SSA debt (excluding South Africa) more than tripled from $60.6 to $205.3 billion. The growth of debt was overwhelmingly from bilateral and multilateral development agency loans. Private debt only grew from $20.8 to $27.5 billion over the same period (Stein, 2013). Therefore, African governments' policy space was dramatically reduced as aid agencies adopted neoliberal loan conditions as the core of their structural adjustment programmes.

The growth of FDI and remittances led to a decline in the dependence of aid for foreign exchange after 2000. By 2007, the ratio of FDI and remittances to ODA reached 1.7 from only 0.13 in 1990. On the surface, SSA countries in 2015–19 had access to five to seven times the amount of foreign exchange annually from FDI compared to 2000, and it had generally risen at rates higher than imports. For example, the ratio of FDI to imports almost doubled to 13 per cent between 2000 and 2015 (UNCTAD, 2021).

Hypothetically, FDI could be a major source of investment in building health sector services and good capacities, but in practice this has not been the case. The outbreak of COVID-19 has generated renewed interest in this subject. The Organisation for Economic Co-operation and Development (OECD) published a study on the impact of FDI on the resilience of health systems for a 2020 roundtable on investment and sustainable development. In 2004, greenfield investment (foreign direct investment building operations from the ground up) in non-OECD countries in healthcare infrastructure and services, pharma, medical devices and biotechnology was only

Table 3.1: Personal remittances, ODA and FDI in SSA 1990–2019 ($ millions)*

Year	1990	2000	2010	2014	2015	2016	2017	2018	2019
Remit	2,363	4,801	31,657	39,680	42,190	38,618	42,330	48,819	48,776
FDI	1,162	6,875	32909	44,275	44,342	30,788	27,581	30,948	31,378
ODA	28,114	17,993	43698	44,509	46,235	47,473	53,365	52,294	52,432
R+F/O	.13	.65	1.5	1.9	1.9	1.5	1.3	1.5	1.5

*ODA are grants from bilateral and multilateral sources and the grant equivalent of soft or concessional loans (eg, the lower the interest rate and longer the payback terms the higher the ODA). It also includes other official flows (OOF). Remittances; FDI are net inflows.

Source: OECD, 2021; World Bank, 2021a; World Bank, 2021b

1.5 per cent of the total, with none of it going to SSA countries (OECD, 2020). By 2019, the total had almost reached 2 per cent with only a small fraction of it going to SSA. So which countries and sectors have attracted most of the FDI?

Jomo and Von Arnim (2012) illustrate the overwhelming focus of FDI on the oil and gas sector historically using data from 1970 to 2006. In the 1970s, one country, Nigeria, Africa's largest oil producer, received 35.4 per cent of all the FDI to SSA. Largely due to the plummeting price of oil in the 1980s, it dropped to only 3 per cent of the total before rising in the 1990s to a dominating 40.6 per cent of all SSA FDI. In the 2000–06 period, it fell to 21.7 per cent, but the sector was 47 per cent of the total when including other oil producers (Equatorial Guinea, Chad, Angola and Sudan). Little has changed. In 2016, 70 per cent of SSA FDI (excluding South Africa) went to oil- and gas-producing countries in SSA (UNCTAD, 2021). The structure of trade reflects the structural impact of FDI, with fuel exports rising from 39.8 per cent of total exports in 1995 to 71.4 per cent of total exports in 2008 before falling slightly to 62.7 per cent in 2014. This helped push countries into greater reliance on unprocessed raw materials, which went from 87.6 per cent of exports in 1987 to 92.2 per cent in 2010 and 92.3 per cent in 2014 before declining to 90 per cent in 2018 (SSA excluding South Africa) (UNCTAD, 2022).

The rise of remittances, in contrast, provides considerably more flexibility as local recipients convert foreign exchange to local currencies, potentially leading to a rise in foreign exchange reserves. The indirect structural impact is uncertain though. A good deal of research has focused on the impact on poverty, inequality and infant mortality based on evidence that remittances go towards higher consumption, house construction, healthcare and educational expenditures. Ratha et al (2012) provide data on the use of remittances for five African countries. In all cases, the majority of funds were allocated to these four categories. However, some studies illustrate increases in GDP and financial development, indicating the possibility of improvements in investment, though there is evidence imports also rise, which could counter some of the gains in reserves (Tah and McMillan, 2019; Letsoalo and Thobeka, 2020). Overall, there is little evidence that FDI and remittances have helped to structurally prepare African countries for COVID-19, though clearly transfers have helped families cope with the economic shocks arising from the pandemic (Akim et al, 2021). There are also other important new sources of finance, including Chinese lending and sovereign debt bonds.

Although bonds denominated in local currencies are issued routinely by most SSA countries, no SSA country except South Africa had issued a Eurobond for many years until the Seychelles sold a $200 million Eurodollar bond in September 2006. The following year, Ghana became the first heavily indebted poor country to issue sovereign bonds on international markets. As indicated in Table 3.2, by the end of 2021, 17 different SSA countries had participated in the Eurobond markets with a gross value of $73 billion (not including South Africa). The funds have been used for a variety of different purposes, including increasing the bargaining power of countries with the IMF.

Governments have used funds from bond issues to expand their reserves or engage in fiscal expansion. Seychelles used its 2006 Eurobond issue to increase its foreign currency reserves. In Namibia, a 2011 bond issue successfully financed a stimulus programme aimed at reducing the unemployment rate. In most cases, funds have been used for infrastructural projects, which are, by their very nature, expansionary and implicitly countercyclical when undertaken during a period of slow economic growth. Therefore, they have bought African countries flexibility to avoid the procyclical policies of the IMF during economic downturns (Stein, 2015). COVID-19 and Zambia's default on payments in October 2020 curtailed the ability to tap these markets. There were only three offerings in 2020, though there had been recovery to pre-COVID-19 levels in late 2021.

Table 3.2: SSA sovereign bond issues excluding South Africa, millions of USD, 2006–21

Countries	2006–09	2010–14	2015	2016	2017	2018	2019	2020	2021	Total
Angola		1,000	1,500				3,000			5,500
Benin							567		1,803	2,370
Cameroon			750						700	1,450
Congo, DRC	478									478
Cote d'Iviore		3,250	1,000		1,875	1,700		1,191	850	9,866
Ethiopia		1,000								1,000
Gabon	1,000	1,500						1,000		3,500
Ghana	750	1,750	1,000	750		2,000	3,000	3,000	3,025	15,275
Kenya		2,750				2,000	2,100		1,000	7850
Mozam		850								850
Namibia		500								500
Nigeria		1,500			4,800	5,368			3,000	14,668

Table 3.2: SSA sovereign bond issues excluding South Africa, millions of USD, 2006–21 (continued)

Countries	2006–09	2010–14	2015	2016	2017	2018	2019	2020	2021	Total
Rwanda		400							620	1,020
Senegal	200	1,000			1000	2000			800	5,000
Seychelles	200	168								368
Tanzania		600								600
Zambia		1,750	1,250							3,000
Total	2,628	18,018	5,500	750	7,675	13,068	8,667	5,191	11,798	73,295

Source: Olabisi and Stein, 2015; Cytonn (various years)

Table 3.3: Chinese lending to African governments and state-owned enterprises

Chinese lender	Year lender provided first loan in Africa	Number of loans signed 2000–19	Gross value of loan commitments 2000–19 (in US$ billion)
Chinese government	1960	212	3.0
China Exim Bank	1995	607	86.2
Suppliers' credits from Chinese firms	2000	64	10.5
Chinese commercial banks and syndicated loans	2001	66	16.6
China Development Bank	2007	166	37.1
Total		1,115	153.4

Source: Brautigam et al, 2020, updated from SAIS, 2021

Table 3.3 presents data on the Chinese loans to SSA, which has provided another important source of lending. Between 2000 and 2020, the total was $159.9 billion. The overwhelming focus is on infrastructure, with $108.2 billion or just under 68 per cent of the total going to transportation ($46.8), power ($40.5), information and communications ($13.5) and water ($7.4). The largest area that is non-infrastructural focus is mining ($18) (SAIS, 2021).

Brautigam (2019) points to the importance of infrastructure in paving the way for structural transformation. However, lending to expand the important area of manufacturing capacity has been much more limited in part due to the movement away from state-owned manufacturing in the adjustment period and after, which has instead emphasized privatization. There have been a few exceptions since 1995, including the building of refineries in Sudan, Chad and Niger; cement factories in Chad, Ethiopia, Eritrea and Republic of the Congo; sugar factories in Ethiopia and Sudan; and agro-industrial milling projects in Zambia and Mozambique. Angola borrowed funds for the expansion of state farms to produce grains.

Loans from China have also buttressed existing structures. In some cases, they have been secured and are paid off from resource revenue. For example, the Chinese loan to Ghana for the Bui Dam was secured with revenue from the export of cocoa to a Chinese company. There were also income streams tied to resources in the Democratic Republic of the Congo, Angola, Equatorial Guinea, Sudan and Congo. Ethiopia used sesame seed sales to China to pay for loans. Chinese loans have also taken the form of sales of manufacturing goods from China to raise local funds for Chinese-financed projects (Brautigam, 2019). Even with all these loans, however, the structure of trade between China and Africa has not changed and looks little different from the broader trade structure. Between 2014 and 2019, 96 per cent of exports from SSA to China were in primary commodities, with 60 per cent in fuels. Imports were also overwhelmingly in manufacturing goods (77 per cent of the total). The trade deficit average with China is $12 billion per year (UNCTAD, 2021).

Despite the importance of these inflows, a broader view of global trends shows that African economies are increasingly excluded from the global economy. In 2019, while the value of Africa's total trade was 106 times higher than in 1950, the continent's share in world trade had declined over the period from 6 per cent to a meagre 2 per cent. And while FDI inflows into Africa grew 35 times between 1970 and 2019, Africa's share of world FDI dropped from 10 per cent to 3 per cent (UNCTAD, 2021). Therefore, while the increasing inflows in absolute terms may suggest that Africa is increasing its integration with the global economy, the continent today actually comprises a smaller role than before independence.

African economies remain subject to a host of other structural inequalities in the global financial architecture. Among these are the failure of an international system to effectively supply liquidity to African economies in moments of global financial crises; the inability to stop the flow of illicit finances and capital flight out of African economies (Ndikumana and Boyce, 2022); the inability to stop tax evasion and tax avoidance schemes that deprive African economies of their due taxes (Sight News, 2021); and the inability to provide an international system for an orderly workout of sovereign debt restructuring following debt crises. All these aspects of the current global system – from the neoliberal development model that undermines structural transformation and development, to the aid, trade and global financial systems – leave African economies at a major disadvantage. The systems collectively undermine the ability of African economies to build domestic tax bases that are capable of financing the necessary increases in long-term public investments in health and education infrastructure. As we have witnessed during the COVID-19 crisis and its economic fallout, such a context has left African economies unable to effectively address health crises, with significant consequences for human health and the sustainability of development.

Notes

[1] See www.africacdc.org/covid-19-vaccination.
[2] We would define the vicious cycle of commodity dependence as one where being dependent on commodities creates the conditions that keep economies dependent on commodities – for example, commodity producers are price takers, which creates boom and bust cycles while making it impossible to transcend the reliance on commodities.
[3] See for example Stein (2008, chapter 3) for a summary of the empirical literature to that point.

References

Akim, A. Ayivod, F. and Kouton, J. (2021) 'Do remittances mitigate COVID-19 employment shock on food insecurity? Evidence from Nigeria', *Humanities and Social Sciences* (HAL-0397425). Available from: https://hal.archives-ouvertes.fr/hal-03207425

Brautigam, D. (2019) 'Chinese loans and African structural change', in J. Lin and A. Oquabay (eds), *China–Africa and an Economic Transformation*, Oxford: Oxford University Press, 129–46.

Brautigam, D., Huang, Y. and Acker, K. (2020) 'Risky business: new data on Chinese loans and Africa's debt problem', SAIS, China–Africa Research Initiative (CARI). Briefing Paper no 3.

Cytonn (various years) 'Sub-Saharan African eurobonds: quarterly reports'. Available from: https://cytonn.com

Jomo, K.S. and von Arnim, R. (2012) 'Economic liberalization and constraints to development in Sub-Saharan Africa', in A. Noman, K. Botchwey, H. Stein and J. Stiglitz (eds), *Good Growth and Governance in Africa: Rethinking Development Strategies*, Oxford: Oxford University Press, 499–535.

Letsoalo, T. and Thobeka, N. (2020) 'Do remittances influence trade in South Africa?', *African Journal of Business and Economic Research*, 15(3) (September): 71–90.

Loscher, A. (2022) 'Being poor in the current monetary system: implication of foreign exchange shortage for African economics and possible solutions', in M. Ben Gadha, F. Kaboub, K. Koddenbrock, I. Mahmoud and N. Samba Sylla (eds), *Economic and Monetary Sovereignty in 21st Century Africa*, London: Pluto Press, 259–83.

Mhone, G. (1995) 'Dependency and underdevelopment: the limits of structural adjustment programmes and towards a pro-active state-led development strategy', *African Development Review*, 7(2): 51–85.

Mkandawire, T. (2001) 'Thinking about developmental states in Africa', *Cambridge Journal of Economics*, 25(3): 289–313.

Ndikumana, L. and Boyce, J.K. (eds) (2022) *On the Trail of Capital Flight from Africa: The Takers and the Enablers*, Oxford: Oxford University Press.

OECD (2020) 'Can FDI improve the resilience of health systems?', Paris: OECD.

OECD (2021) 'OECD-stat'. Available from: https://stats.oecd.org

Olabisi, M. and Stein, H. (2015) 'African sovereign bond issues: do African governments pay more to borrow?', *Journal of African Trade*, 2(1–2): 87–109.

Ortiz, I. and Cummins, M. (2021) 'Global austerity alert: looming budget cuts in 2021 −25 and alternative pathways', Initiative for Policy Dialogue, World Paper, April. Available from: https://policydialogue.org/files/publications/papers/Global-Austerity-Alert-Ortiz-Cummins-2021-final.pdf

Ostry, J.D., Loungani, P. and Furceri, D. (2016) 'Neoliberalism: oversold?', *Finance & Development*, 53(2) (June).

Ratha, D., Mohapatra, S., Özden, C., Plaza, S., Shaw, W. Shimeles, A. (2012) 'Leveraging migration for Africa remittances, skills, and investments', Washington: World Bank

SAIS, China Africa Research Initiative (2021) 'Chinese loans to Africa data base'. Available from: https://chinaafricaloandata.bu.edu

Sight News (2021) 'African civil society organisations: call for rejection of OECD/G20 Global Tax Deal', 31 October.

Stein, H. (2008) *Beyond the World Bank Agenda: An Institutional Approach to Development*, Chicago: University of Chicago Press.

Stein, H. (2013) 'Africa and the perversities of international capital flows', in *International Papers in Political Economy*, Basingstoke: Palgrave Macmillan.

Stein, H. (2015) 'Africa and the Great Recession: the dynamics of growth sustainability', in *International Papers in Political Economy*, Basingstoke: Palgrave Macmillan.

Stein, H. and Nissanke, M. (1999) 'Structural adjustment and the African crisis: a theoretical appraisal', *Eastern Economic Journal*, 25(4): 399–420.

Tah, K. and McMillan, D. (2019) 'Remittances and financial access: evidence from Sub-Saharan Africa', *Cogent Economics and Finance*, 7(1).

UNCTAD (2019) 'Commodity dependence: a twenty-year perspective'. Available from: https://unctad.org/en/Publications Library/ditccom2019d2_en.pdf

UNCTAD (2021) 'World investment report', Geneva: UNCTAD.

UNCTAD (2022) 'UNCTADSTAT'. Available from: https://unctad.org/statistics

World Bank (2021a) 'Personal remittances received, SSA'. Available from: https://data.worldbank.org/indicator/BX.TRF.PWKR.CD.DT?locations=ZG

World Bank (2021b) 'Foreign direct investment, net inflows, SSA'. Available from: https://data.worldbank.org/indicator/BX.KLT.DINV.CD.WD?locations=ZG

FOUR

COVID-19 Vaccine Inequality and Global Development: A Primer

Rory Horner

COVID-19 vaccine development, manufacture and supply is a triumph yet also an ongoing tragedy for global development. COVID-19 vaccines were brought to use in unprecedentedly quick terms. Billions of doses have been manufactured and administered, helping mitigate the impact of a devastating pandemic. However, despite widespread discursive acknowledgement that 'it will not be over anywhere until it's over everywhere', the availability and accessibility of COVID-19 vaccines has been grossly inequitable – challenging what the world needs economically, ethically and epidemiologically.

A brief assortment of facts provides an initial glimpse into the scale of the inequalities related to COVID-19 vaccines. By the time more than 50 per cent of people in Europe and the United States had been fully vaccinated (11 September 2021), only 3.4 per cent of those in Africa were, with many health workers still not fully unvaccinated (*The Guardian*, 2021). By 1 January 2022, the number of booster doses administered in high-income countries (300.6 million) was just over quadruple that of first doses in low-income countries (LICs) (74.8 million). Some vaccines have even been sent from places with low-vaccination rates to those with much higher ones – such as 5 million doses from India to the UK in March 2021 – at a time when the UK had administered more than 23 times the number of doses per 100 people than India (OWID, 2021).

This chapter unpacks the nature of, and factors underlying, COVID-19 vaccine inequality as a global development challenge. It argues that high-, and to some extent middle-income, countries have prioritized addressing their own immediate problems – in this case domestic COVID-19 vaccination – but ultimately at the self-defeating expense of addressing global collective challenges and leaving people in LICs behind. In that regard, the case of COVID-19 vaccines may be indicative of wider challenges related to 21st-century global development (Horner, 2020; Oldekop et al, 2020).

Vaccine nationalism and the scramble for COVID-19 vaccines

Once the genetic make-up of COVID-19 was identified from early January 2020, vaccine development began. Although usually taking over ten years (Thanh Le et al, 2020), within the space of a year, the administration of COVID-19 vaccines outside clinical trials had begun. An ideal global distribution of a successful vaccine would prioritize health workers, followed by countries with major outbreaks and then elderly and those particularly at risk (Wouters et al, 2021). However, fears that the distribution of vaccines may not meet that ideal were fuelled both by the case of high-income countries hoarding vaccines for the swine flu (H1N1) pandemic in 2009 (Okonjo-Iweala, 2020) and personal protective equipment (PPE) in the early weeks of the COVID-19 pandemic in 2020 (Dallas et al, 2021).

By the time COVID-19 vaccines began to be widely administered, the initial seeds for inequalities in their distribution were already sown. Key vaccine developers received large amounts of public funding from governments in high-income countries in support of the trial, development and manufacture of their COVID-19 vaccines. In return, those governments booked priority access to those vaccines.

However, such governments have been criticized for not acquiring the rights to manufacturing know-how when investing in research and development (R&D) and thus not obtaining greater rights to potentially force the technology to be shared in the interests of vaccinating the world (Love, 2021).

Although the full details of these funding arrangements are mostly not publicly available, some basic facts illustrate the scale of this support. Most prominently, the United States' Operation Warp Speed, launched on 15 May 2020, took an 'at-risk' approach to support the trials and manufacturing of vaccines that had not yet been approved. More than $1 billion was provided to each of Moderna, Pfizer, Johnson & Johnson, Novavax, AstraZeneca and Sanofi/GlaxoSmithKline for their joint candidate (Bown and Bollyky, 2021). Due to the invocation of the Defense Production Act, manufacturers had to prioritize allocating their capacity to filling US government orders. The funding supported not just the vaccine developer (for example, Moderna), but also other firms that would play key roles in the supply chain. In another example, the UK government announced spending of more than £2.9 billion from May to October 2020 for priority access to 267 million doses (Bown and Bollyky, 2021: 37). The European Union (EU) also provided direct financing support, for example to BioNTech and CureVac. Other countries, including Australia, Canada, Japan and South Korea, bought directly from vaccine developers. Over-ordering was widespread and justified on the basis of uncertainty over which vaccines would be successfully developed and the need to spread risk (Wintour, 2021).

Once these vaccines received initial regulatory approvals, they were rolled out in national programmes by countries that had pre-ordered. Vaccination programmes in Europe and the United States began at the end of 2020/beginning of 2021 with the Pfizer/BioNTech and Moderna vaccines – both of which are mRNA vaccines. However, the demand for vaccines in already well-vaccinated countries has not ended with an initial two doses for all adults – the original definition of fully vaccinated for most vaccines, except single-dose regimens – as vaccination programmes have expanded with booster shots and doses for children. Israel was the first country to start booster shots, in July 2021, and was joined in the following two months by many other high-income countries. However, they and others planning booster doses were criticized by the World Health Organization's (WHO) Director General Tedros Adhanom Ghebreyesus, who called in early August 2021 for a moratorium on such programmes, while the WHO Africa Director said that booster shots 'make a mockery of African recovery' (Dahir, 2021). COVID-19 vaccination programmes were also expanded in the second half of 2021 to include children in high(er)-income countries, although such allocation before doses have been administered in low(er)-income countries has been criticized by the WHO's Director General and Oxford University's Sarah Gilbert (one of the original developers of the Oxford/AstraZeneca vaccine). Such programmes and the possibility of further boosters undermine any idea that already highly vaccinated countries no longer need more COVID-19 vaccines and may continue to delay availability of doses for other countries.

It was not just high-income countries that developed, manufactured and initially accessed COVID-19 vaccines, however, with China and Russia prominently developing their own candidates with state support. On 31 December 2020, China gave conditional approval for general use of a Sinopharm vaccine, produced by Beijing Bio-Institute of Biological Products Co Ltd, a subsidiary of China National Biotec Group. A second Chinese vaccine, Sinovac's CoronaVac, was approved for general use on 6 February 2021. Both Sinopharm and Sinovac vaccines are inactivated vaccines (a long-established approach to boosting the body's immunity by exposing it to killed viral particles). China's domestic vaccination programmes, using both vaccines, passed the milestones of 1 billion COVID-19 doses administered on 19 June 2021 and 2 billion on 26 August 2021. In Russia, a widespread rollout of its Sputnik V vaccine began in December 2020, and the vaccine was key in Russia reaching 100 million doses administered by 22 October 2021.

A substantial number of COVID-19 vaccines have been exported from China, but largely outside of COVAX and especially to middle-income economies. By 8 October 2021, it was estimated that China had exported 1.1 billion doses (either as bulk substances – the key ingredients for vaccines – or finished doses) to 123 countries (Song, 2021), with Brazil, Pakistan and Iran among the biggest recipients (Mallapaty, 2021). By October 2021, CoronaVac was the most administered COVID-19 vaccine in the world.

Other countries also participated in the manufacture and distribution of COVID-19 vaccines but through technology transfer under license. India's COVID-19 vaccination drive has primarily been driven by a vaccine branded as Covishield, manufactured by the Serum Institute of India (SII) – the world's largest vaccine manufacturer by volume – under license from AstraZeneca. The modified adenovirus vaccine was originally developed at Oxford University. SII did not receive financial support from the Indian government until 2021 (along with Bharat Biotech), although at-risk funding of $300 million from the Bill & Melinda Gates Foundation via GAVI, the Vaccine Alliance, to support supply to COVAX was announced in August and September 2020. Covishield received government approval for emergency use on 3 January, paving the way for the commencement of India's COVID-19 vaccination programme on 16 January 2021. A domestically developed and manufactured vaccine, Bharat Biotech's Covaxin, also received emergency use approval at the same time and inclusion in the country's vaccination programme. While other technology transfer agreements have been made (for example, Hyderabad-based Biological E with Johnson & Johnson) and other Indian companies have attempted developing their own vaccines, SII has played the primary role in India's domestic vaccination programme – producing 88 per cent of the first 1 billion doses administered domestically, a milestone reached on 21 October 2021. However, despite India receiving global praise for the export – especially to neighbouring countries – of more than 60 million vaccines before the end of March 2021, its exports were suspended until October 2021.

South America has also made significant progress on COVID-19 vaccination (Harrison et al, 2022). Indeed, by late August 2021, it had a higher share of vaccinated people than other continents – a position it still held through to April 2022 (the last data update before print) (see Figure 4.1). This was helped mostly by the import of vaccines from China, as well as some local production of vaccines. For example, Brazil has local production of vaccines under license from Oxford/AstraZeneca and Sinovac, while Latin American production also involves a Mexico–Argentina collaboration to co-produce the Oxford/AstraZeneca vaccine and Cuba's domestically developed vaccine.

LICs, and especially Africa, have been left behind on COVID-19 vaccination. This inequality is not just vis-à-vis high-income economies or what are typically classified as countries in the 'Global North', but also vis-à-vis upper middle-income countries, and to a lesser extent vis-à-vis lower-middle-income countries – see Figure 4.2.

COVAX and the struggle for vaccine equity

COVAX (the COVID-19 Vaccine Global Access Facility), the vaccines component of the Access to COVID-19 Tools (ACT), was launched in April 2020 with the aim of promoting equitable access to COVID-19 vaccines. COVAX was created by GAVI (The Global Alliance for Vaccines and Immunization), the WHO and Coalition for Epidemic Preparedness Innovations through *push* financing (supporting pharmaceutical companies' R&D directly) and also employs advanced market commitments as a *pull* mechanism through procurement upon licensure. Its initial aim was to distribute 2

Figure 4.1: Share of people vaccinated against COVID-19, 18 April 2022

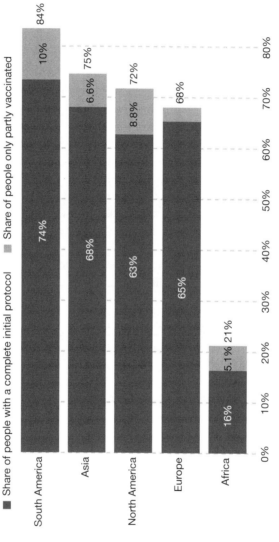

■ Share of people with a complete initial protocol   ■ Share of people only partly vaccinated

Note: Alternative definitions of a full vaccination, for example having been infected with SARS-CoV-2 and having one dose of a two-dose protocol, are ignored to maximize comparability between countries.

Source: Our World in Data (2022)

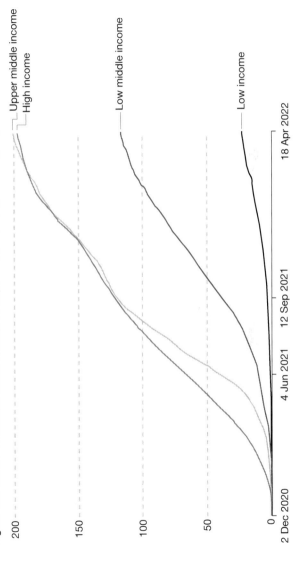

Figure 4.2: COVID-19 vaccine doses administered per 100 people, by income group

Notes: All doses, including boosters, are counted individually. Country income groups are based on the World Bank Classification.

Source: Our World in Data (2022)

billion doses by the end of 2021 (Berkley et al, 2020), sufficient to cover 20 per cent of people in participating countries (that is, enough for high-risk people and healthcare workers). It aimed that all countries would buy-in – some self-financing and others as donor-funded (Shadlen, 2020).

The first COVAX vaccines were delivered relatively early in the overall context of global COVID-19 vaccination, with a batch of AstraZeneca vaccines arriving in Ghana on 24 February 2021. That vaccine received emergency use authorization approval from the WHO on 15 February 2021 – a necessary standard for COVAX procurement. Seth Berkley, CEO of GAVI, noted that the time gap between the administration of first doses of COVID-19 vaccines anywhere and their distribution in 'many countries in the developing world … is extraordinary compared to the historical timeline' (Berkley, 2021).

However, COVAX's push for equitable access has been undermined especially by countries prioritizing national procurement of vaccines and therefore reducing availability for COVAX given the limited overall supply. High-, and then middle-income, countries pursued bilateral procurement deals, seeking to have many more doses than the coverage of 20 per cent of their populations they could aim for with COVAX (Shadlen, 2020). The WHO's Director General has consistently pleaded for more doses to be given to COVAX. In April 2021, for example, he suggested that while leaders of the world's biggest economies had provided some financial support for COVAX, they had also undermined it by hoarding supplies (Ghebreyesus, 2021b).

COVAX was particularly hit by a shortfall on the projected delivery from SII, which was initially expected to be its biggest supplier. Under license from AstraZeneca, the Indian vaccine manufacturer was projected to supply over 1 billion doses of COVAX's initial (January 2021) forecast of 2.3 billion doses by the end of 2021. However, this target was not met as India's production capacity was directed towards supplying its domestic vaccination programme from late March 2021 as India's second wave of COVID-19 materialized. Exports from SII to COVAX did not resume until 26 November 2021. Heavily linked to this shortfall from India, it took until 15 January 2022 for COVAX to reach 1 billion doses shipped (UNICEF, 2022).

COVAX's struggles are also because of regulatory and availability issues with other COVID-19 vaccines. Novavax's vaccine was expected to play a key role in COVAX's 2021 supply but did not receive its first approval from a major regulator – the European Medicines Agency – until late December 2021. COVAX did not initially invest much in the Pfizer or Moderna mRNA vaccines (a relatively recent type of vaccine that instructs cells in the body to make a protein to trigger an immune response), with the suitability of these vaccines for LICs questioned due to extremely low storage requirements (*The Economist*, 2021). Delays in regulatory approval meant that COVAX procurement from Sinopharm (approved by WHO, 7 May 2021, first COVAX delivery 11 August 2021) and Sinovac (approved by WHO, 2 June 2021, first COVAX doses delivered 31 August 2021) had been limited in 2021, while Russia's Sputnik V had still not been approved by the WHO by April 2022.

The vaccines that have been central to immunization programmes in high-income countries have not been made widely available in LICs. An analysis of the first nine months of 2021 shows that Pfizer/BioNTech and Moderna only sold 1 per cent and 3 per cent of their supply to COVAX, while Johnson & Johnson sold 25 per cent and AstraZeneca 19 per cent. Remarkably, of the first 2 billion COVID-19 Pfizer vaccines shipped, only 15.4 million went to LICs (Amnesty International, 2021).

Donations of doses – either direct or via COVAX – have been slow and insufficient to address the extent of vaccine inequality. Following a trickle of smaller donation pledges through the first half of 2021, at the G7 Summit in June 2021, the United States pledged an additional 500 million doses (beyond the 87.5 million earlier) and the UK 100 million – both for low- and middle-income countries (LMICs) by 2022 (Padma, 2021). On 22 July 2021, the European Commission announced that 'Team Europe' (the EU and all 27 member states) would share 200 million COVID-19 vaccines, mostly through COVAX, with LMICs by the end of 2021. Despite the rhetoric of the importance of vaccinating the world, substantial issues have arisen with donations. Sharing doses sooner is more impactful than later, but often there have been substantial delays between promises made to share vaccines and their actual delivery (for example, Newey et al, 2021, 9 July; see also Our World in Data, 2021). Indeed, AVAT (Africa Vaccine Acquisitions Trust), Africa CDC (Africa Centres for Diseases Control and Prevention) and COVAX issued a statement (29 November 2021) saying that 'the majority of the donations to-date have been ad hoc, provided with little notice and short shelf lives. This has made it extremely challenging for countries to plan vaccination campaigns and increase absorptive capacity … Countries need predictable and reliable supply' (Africa CDC, 2021; also see COVAX, 2021).

An ongoing challenge for, and portal on, global development

Global COVID-19 vaccine inequality is an enormous challenge. To date, the pursuit of perceived national self-interest by high-, and to some extent middle-, income countries has overridden what the world needs in terms of managing and ending the pandemic and minimizing the economic impact. While such countries have prioritized access to vaccines for more vulnerable populations domestically, they have not acted to protect the most vulnerable in a global context. The major multilateral initiative to promote vaccine equity, COVAX, has received some funding but has struggled to access doses – being directly undermined by bilateral deals and pre-booking of doses. As a result, LICs and some lower-middle-income countries continue to be left behind in terms of COVID-19 vaccine access. The continuation of vaccination programmes in already relatively highly vaccinated countries – to include children and booster doses – serves to reinforce these inequalities.

The extent of COVID-19 vaccine inequality is not just a "catastrophic moral failure", as termed by the WHO Director General, but is disastrous economically as well as epidemiologically. Various studies have pointed to ongoing economic costs for all countries due to the ongoing pandemic. An International Monetary Fund (IMF) study in May 2021 estimated that immediate investment of $50 billion in COVID-19 vaccination would yield $9 trillion (or a return on investment of 267 per cent per year over four years) in growth by 2025. The IMF's Managing Director, Kristalina Georgieva, touted COVID-19 vaccination as 'the highest return on public investment in modern history' (Kristof, 2021). The heads of the IMF, World Bank, WHO and World Trade Organization (WTO) warned in July 2021 that inequity in COVID-19 vaccine distribution would hold back global economic recovery (Wintour, 2021). Epidemiologically, WHO has stated that 'vaccine inequality is the world's biggest obstacle to ending this pandemic and recovering from COVID-19' (WHO, 2021a). Having substantial unvaccinated populations increases the possibility of new, vaccine-resistant mutations emerging (Ghebreyesus, 2021a). In light of the identification of the Omicron variant in November 2021, South African President Cyril Ramaphosa simply warned: "[V]accine inequality cannot be allowed to continue … Until everyone is vaccinated, we should expect that more variants will emerge" (Ramaphosa, 2021).

COVID-19 vaccine inequality can be addressed by expanding the pie of available vaccines and/or by a better distribution of that pie. The production of COVID-19 vaccines has been scaled up enormously by the original developers of those vaccines and the licensing of their technology to manufacturing partners. The People's Vaccine campaign, WHO, Unitaid and the South Centre, among others, have advocated expanding the pie of vaccines and other COVID-19-related products through a TRIPS (Trade-Related Aspects of Intellectual Property Rights) waiver, originally proposed by India and South Africa to the WTO in October 2020. While the example of how patent-free antiretrovirals transformed treatment for people living with HIV-AIDS is frequently pointed to, it is unclear what – if any – effect waiving patents would have on the supply of vaccines (for example, Hotez et al, 2021). Vaccines do not have a codified recipe that others can replicate (Gates, 2021), and the cooperation of the originator is required for scaling up – otherwise trials would have to start from the beginning (Science and Technology Committee, 2021). Jamie Love, director of Knowledge Ecology International and prominent campaigner on patents, has thus said that "know-how is the bigger problem than patent rights in the shorter run" (Lerner, 2020). However, mechanisms to force companies to do this are limited, especially as a clause on sharing know-how was not required by many governments when providing initial funding. As the COVID-19 pandemic continues and volumes of vaccines have increased, the weight of the access problem has shifted even more clearly in terms of maldistribution being the key problem. A much better allocation of the growing pie of COVID-19 vaccines would be the fastest way to increase the number of vaccines available to LICs. This requires increased doses (and prompt delivery) for COVAX and donation pledges being delivered promptly, as the WHO (2021b) has repeatedly asked for, and *Médecins Sans Frontières* (MSF, 2021) has also argued for.

Ultimately, the case, and difficulties of, COVID-19 vaccines may point to wider struggles in addressing global development problems. We live in a world that faces several interconnected development problems that cut across both the Global North and Global South, rather than just being located within the latter. Examples include, notably, climate change, but also addressing global inequality and combatting tax avoidance, which simply cannot be done on a national basis alone. As well as interconnected issues, there are also shared issues such as relative poverty, social protection, decent work, effective states and so on. Although such challenges may relate to all countries, they are extremely uneven in their impacts. Moreover, as with COVID-19 vaccines, the solutions are also likely to cut across Global North and South relations with multidirectional learning and collaboration in the global collective interest required. Lessons must be learnt from the failures currently experienced from COVID-19 vaccination to not just better address the ongoing pandemic, or future crises, but for a wider range of global development issues. Coordination is needed for both COVID-19 vaccination and climate change (Pai and Olatunbosun-Alakija, 2021). A danger is that higher-income countries prioritize their own populations at the expense of the most vulnerable globally and everyone's interests. The current case has demonstrated how the pursuit of perceived self-interest is not just bad for the world as a whole but also for the original architects of that self-interest.

References

Africa CDC, AVAT and COVAX (2021) 'Joint statement on dose donations of COVID-19 vaccines to African countries', 29 November. Available from: https://www.gavi.org/news/media-room/joint-statement-dose-donations-covid-19-vaccines-afri can-countries

Amnesty International (2021) 'Despite the rhetoric, Pfizer's failures continue to fuel human rights COVID-19 crisis', 11 November. Available from: https://www.amnesty.org/en/latest/news/2021/ 11/covid-19-new-research-reveals-pfizer-is-making-misleading-claims-about-fair-distribution-of-vaccines

Berkley, S. (2021) 'Vaccinating the world: from mass production to last mile delivery', World Economic Forum, 26 January. Available from: https://www.weforum.org/events/the-davos-age nda-2021/sessions/vaccinating-the-world-from-mass-product ion-to-last-mile-delivery

Berkley, S., Hatchett, R. and Swaminathan, S. (2020) 'The fastest way out of the pandemic', Project Syndicate, 15 July. Available from: https://www.project-syndicate.org/commentary/covid-19-vaccine-cooperation-covax-by-seth-berkley-et-al-2020-07?utm _source=twitter&utm_medium=organic-social&utm_campa ign=page-posts-july20&utm_post-type=link&utm_format= 16:9&utm_creative=link-image&utm_post-date=2020-07-15

Bown, C. and Bollyky, T.J. (2021) 'How COVID-19 vaccine supply chains emerged in the midst of a pandemic', Working Paper 21–12, Washington: Peterson Institute for International Economics.

COVAX (2021) 'COVAX joint statement: call to action to equip COVAX to deliver 2 billion doses in 2021', UNICEF. Available from: https://www.unicef.org/press-releases/covax-joint-statem ent-call-action-equip-covax-deliver-2-billion-doses-2021-0

Dahir, A.L. (2021) 'Booster shots "make a mockery of African recovery"', *The New York Times*, 19 August. Available from: https://www.nytimes.com/2021/08/19/world/africa/afr ica-vaccine-booster-shots.html

Dallas, M.P., Horner, R. and Li, L. (2021) 'The mutual constraints of states and global value chains during COVID-19: the case of personal protective equipment', *World Development*, 139: 105324.

The Economist (2021) 'The great task – vaccinating the world', 9 January. Available from: https://www.economist.com/briefing/ 2021/01/09/the-great-task

Gates, B. (2021) 'Next time, we can close the vaccine gap much faster', 13 October. Available from: https://www.gatesnotes. com/Health/Closing-the-vaccine-gap?WT.mc_id=20211013100 000_vaccine-gap_BG-TW_&WT.tsrc=BGTW

Ghebreyesus, T.A. (2021a) 'Vaccine nationalism harms everyone and protects no one', *Foreign Policy*, 2 February. Available from: https://foreignpolicy.com/2021/02/02/vaccine-national ism-harms-everyone-and-protects-no-one

Ghebreyesus, T.A. (2021b) 'I run the W.H.O. and I know that rich countries must make a choice', *The New York Times*, 22 April. Available from: https://www.nytimes.com/2021/04/22/opinion/ who-covid-vaccines.html

The Guardian (2021) '*The Guardian* view on vaccine justice: what the world needs now', 16 November. Available from: https:// www.theguardian.com/commentisfree/2021/nov/16/the-guard ian-view-on-vaccine-justice-what-the-world-needs-now

Harrison, C., Horwitz, L. and Zissis, C. (2022) 'Timeline: tracking Latin America's road to vaccination', AS/COA, 6 June. Available from: https://www.as-coa.org/articles/timeline-tracking-latin- americas-road-vaccination

Horner, R. (2020) 'Towards a new paradigm of global development? Beyond the limits of international development', *Progress in Human Geography*, 44(3): 415–36.

Hotez, P.J., Botazzi, M. and Yadav, P. (2021) 'Producing a vaccine requires more than a patent', *Foreign Affairs*, 10 May. Available from: https://www.foreignaffairs.com/articles/united-states/ 2021-05-10/producing-vaccine-requires-more-patent

Kristof, N. (2021) 'Vaccinate the world! The best investment ever', *The New York Times*, 26 May. Available from: https://www.nyti mes.com/2021/05/26/opinion/biden-covid-vaccine-world.html

Lerner, S. (2020) 'World faces COVID-19 "vaccine apartheid"', The Intercept, 31 December. Available from: https://theinterc ept.com/2020/12/31/covid-vaccine-countries-scarcity-access

Love, J. (2021) 'Buying know-how to scale vaccine manufacturing', Medium, 10 March. Available from: https://jamie-love.medium. com/buying-know-how-to-scale-vaccine-manufacturing-586bd b304a36

Mallapaty, S. (2021) 'China's COVID vaccines have been crucial – now immunity is waning', *Nature*, 598: 398–9.

MSF (Médecins Sans Frontières) (2021) 'COVID-19 vaccine redistribution to save lives now', 7 October. Available from: https://msfaccess.org/covid-19-vaccine-redistribution-save-lives-now

Newey, S., Gulland, A. and Rigby, J. (2021) 'All talk, no jabs: the reality of global vaccine diplomacy', *The Telegraph*, 9 July. Available from: https://www.telegraph.co.uk/global-health/science-and-disease/talk-no-jabs-reality-global-vaccine-diplomacy

Okonjo-Iweala, N. (2020) 'Finding a vaccine is only the first step: no one will be safe until the whole world is safe', *Foreign Affairs*, 30 April. Available from: https://www.foreignaffairs.com/articles/world/2020-04-30/finding-vaccine-only-first-step

Oldekop, J.A., Horner, R., Hulme, D., Adhikari, R., Agarwal, B., Alford, M. et al (2020) 'COVID-19 and the case for global development', *World Development*, 134: 105044.

Our World in Data (OWID) (2021) 'Coronavirus (COVID-19) vaccinations'. Available from: https://ourworldindata.org/covid-vaccinations

Padma, T.V. (2021) 'COVID vaccines to reach poorest countries in 2023 – despite recent pledges', *Nature*, 5 July. Available from: https://www.nature.com/articles/d41586-021-01762-w

Pai, M. and Olatunbosun-Alakija, A. (2021) 'Vax the world', *Science*, 374(6571): 1031.

Ramaphosa, C. (2021) 'President Cyril Ramaphosa: address on South Africa's response to Coronavirus COVID-19 pandemic, government of South Africa', 28 November. Available from: https://www.gov.za/speeches/president-cyril-ramaphosa-address-south-africas-response-coronavirus-covid-19-pandemic-28

Science and Technology Committee (2021) 'Oral evidence: UK science, research and technology capability and influence in global disease outbreaks, HC 136', House of Commons, 24 February.

Shadlen, K. (2020) '12 days of global health: power and the reproduction of global inequalities', LSE Blog, 14 December. Available from: https://blogs.lse.ac.uk/globalhealth/2020/12/14/12-days-of-global-health-power-and-the-reproduction-of-global-inequalities

Song, W. (2021) 'COVID-19 vaccines: has China made more than other countries combined? BBC News, 10 October. Available from: https://www.bbc.co.uk/news/58808889

Thanh Le, T., Zacharias, A., Kumar, A., Gómez Román, R. Tollefsen, S., Saville, M. et al (2020) 'The COVID-19 vaccine development landscape', Nature Reviews Drug Discovery. Available from: https://www.nature.com/articles/d41573-020-00073-5

UNICEF (2022) 'COVID-19 vaccine market dashboard'. Available from: https://www.unicef.org/supply/covid-19-vaccine-market-dashboard

WHO (2021a) 'Vaccine inequity undermining global economic recovery', 22 July. Available from: https://www.who.int/news/item/22-07-2021-vaccine-inequity-undermining-global-economic-recovery

WHO (2021b) 'Joint statement of the Multilateral Leaders Taskforce on scaling COVID-19 tools – a crisis of vaccine inequity', 27 August. Available from: https://www.who.int/news/item/27-08-2021-joint-statement-of-the-multilateral-leaders-taskforce-on-scaling-covid-19-tools

Wintour, P. (2021) 'Boris Johnson to pledge surplus Covid vaccine to poorer countries at G7', *The Guardian*, 18 February. Available from: https://www.theguardian.com/world/2021/feb/18/boris-johnson-to-pledge-surplus-covid-vaccine-to-poorer-countries-at-g7

Wouters, O.J., Shadlen, K., Konrad-Salcher, M., Pollard, A.J., Larson, H.J., Teerawattananon, Y. et al (2021) 'Challenges in ensuring global access to COVID-19 vaccines: production, affordability, allocation, and deployment', *The Lancet*, 397(10278): 1023–34.

PART II

Policy Context

FIVE

Corporate Social Responsibility in the Time of Pandemic: An Indian Overview

Sujay Ghosh and Naveen Das

Corporate Social Responsibility (CSR) means 'various self-regulatory mechanisms and controls which corporate management might initiate to ensure, or seem to ensure, compliance with ethical standards, international norms and the true spirit of the law, in transactions with all stakeholders' (Corporate Reform Collective, 2014: 52). Stakeholders include direct clients, shareholders, employees and others who are directly or indirectly affected by their operations. Ethical standards apply to labour laws, environment and the quality of the goods and services they provide. In India, the importance of inclusive growth has been widely recognized as an agenda for development, particularly after it was stunted by two centuries of colonial rule. In their various endeavours and growth processes, both the state and industry have expressed commitments to include those sections of the society that had hitherto been excluded from the mainstream of development. CSR in India has to be understood in this context: as an instrument for integrating social, environmental and human development concerns in the entire value chain of corporate business. This chapter will look at how CSR has influenced responses to the pandemic as it spread in India.

Corporate Social Responsibility: beyond charity

CSR is different from philanthropy or charity – it reflects the way business pays back to society, because it receives inputs like raw materials and labour, and output such as after-sales profit from society. Over the last two decades, various stakeholders started demanding responsibility and accountability from firms. Businesses also felt the necessity to win people's trust and confidence, and hence there has been greater sensitivity to sociopolitical issues, particularly in the context of rising inequalities, environmental degradation and forced displacement. As a result, many firms are paying specific attention to CSR. In the long run, they also reap benefits: by making small investments to sensitize employees on recycling waste, energy efficiency and managing water, firms are also able to cut their costs of production. Indeed, a company could save their own resources and may earn additional profits from the sale of its 'waste'.[1] In addition, CSR enables firms to reach many new people through social activities, thus enhancing its potential customer-base (Agarwal, 2008). CSR is also a sound business strategy – the promulgation of a corporate code of conduct has been among global business's preferred strategies for quelling popular discontent with corporate power. CSR discourse has accelerated the development of alternative business forms that prioritize sustainability and social justice over simply maximizing profit (Rowe, 2005). CSR activism in India has to be understood in this context.

When the Indian state became independent on 15 August 1947, it embarked on a path of massive social and economic restructuring: a democratic constitution was adopted, and many retrogressive social practices and privileges, such as the practice of untouchability and private landlordism, were abolished. A state-led planned economy was adopted to attain rapid all-round and inclusive growth and development, particularly in the fields of heavy engineering, infrastructure and emerging industries, against the backdrop of the limited participation and capacities of the private sector.[2] Within a quarter of a century, by the 1970s, the public sector had come to assume a dominant role in the economy. During the first few decades after independence, India's economy performed sluggishly: derisively termed the 'Hindu rate of growth' (Rodrik and Subramanian, 2004), quite in contrast to the government's mounting expenditure that had increased manifold by then. From the 1980s, in tune with the resurgent neoliberal ethos in many parts of the world, an influential section of Indian public opinion started advocating for privatizing and downsizing the public sector, to allow the market to flourish (Nigam, 2002) – this trend has been criticized as 'Indian Thatcherism' (Vanaik, 1990: 55–8). The public sector earned considerable criticism for being inefficient, corrupt and wasteful for the public exchequer. Many policymakers also favoured a gradual expansion of the private sector while curtailing the public sector.

Private business was allowed more space in the economy from the early 1980s, but since the early 1990s increasing dependence on external financing, particularly from the World Bank and International Monetary Fund (which insisted on pro-business structural reforms and curtailing governmental expenditures), led India to decisively adopt the path of a neoliberal economy. During the same period, the breakup of the Soviet Union had adversely affected both foreign exports and a steady source of defence materiel; the other supplier, the United States insisted on hard currency for defence equipment. Policymakers realized that a healthy reserve of foreign exchange could be earned by increasing exports. By 1994, when the World Trade Organization was established, it became clear that India could no longer escape the reality of being integrated into the global economy (Kohli, 2012: 32–41). During this period, several developing countries, including

India, were projected as a brand: an attractive destination for investment due to their rich cultural heritage, a vast reserve of natural resources and a population capable of producing and consuming substantially (Kaur, 2020). Finally, from the mid-1980s, ambitious information and communication technology policies and programmes were initiated, resulting in India achieving global acclamation in this area. GDP overcame the 'Hindu rate of growth', predominantly by piggybacking on corporate performance. A combination of these factors had resulted in an increasing influence of the corporate sector at India's policymaking levels. The subsequent decade witnessed a higher volume of economic activities, from a state-led welfare regime to the Indian developmental state embracing a decisively free-market economy, under the cumulative influence of liberalization, privatization and globalization. The enhanced influence of the corporate sector was palpable. Apart from generating direct employment, CSR activism also caught popular attention.

Corporate Social Responsibility: the Indian scenario

The globally acclaimed business-insights provider Dun & Bradstreet has classified the top 500 companies in India into 58 categories: ranging from automobile, software, pharmaceutical and metal sectors to hotel and media sectors (Dun & Bradstreet, 2021). Having accessed the websites of 116 companies – the first and the last ones listed in each category – we found that for 74 companies CSR has been clearly and explicitly mentioned, or at least indicated on the landing page of their website, whereas it is not that conspicuous for the remaining 42 companies. Traditionally, CSR in India has been seen as a philanthropic activity, but with the introduction of Section 135 in the Companies Act 2013, India became the first country to have statutorily mandated CSR for companies with a net worth of a minimum Rupees (Rs) 500 crore (1 crore = 10 million), or turnover of a minimum Rs 1,000 crore, or net profit of a minimum Rs 5 crore during the immediately preceding financial year, to spend 2 per cent of the average net profits of the immediately preceding three years on CSR activities. The statute also specifies the methods and scope for CSR projects or programmes and Schedule VII of the Companies Act, 2013 mandates that companies shall indicate, as part of their CSR policy, the activities in areas or subjects, their modalities of execution and monitoring, and treatment of surplus arising out of CSR. Companies must also disclose the content of CSR policies in their annual report and preferably publish it on their website (Ministry of Corporate Affairs, 2014). This legislation, it appears, has created a readily available legal infrastructure for meeting unforeseen crises such as COVID-19.

On 23 March 2020, the Indian government notified businesses that all expenditure incurred on activities related to COVID-19 would be added as permissible avenues for CSR expenditure. These activities related to the promotion of healthcare, including preventive healthcare, sanitation and disaster management (Ministry of Corporate Affairs, 2020). This mandate encouraged the corporate sector to participate in a substantial way in their socially responsible endeavours, showing solidarity with the nation in its war against the pandemic. About 80 per cent of the annual CSR budget of India Inc was allocated to address the pandemic, which is a testimony to the concern the corporate sector has shown during a time of unprecedented adversity. Surveys by global audit firms confirmed that, by and large, there is a general compliance by companies on this front, thus indicating the healthy impact of business entities on the social and economic spheres. CSR budgets are of huge significance in a context where the Indian state, as with governments elsewhere, is trying desperately to grapple with the sudden and continuing onslaught of COVID-19.

Since early 2020, the Indian government, like their counterparts in other countries, have faced extreme challenges stemming from the reach and devastating effects of the pandemic. At times, the Indian state appeared quite unprepared to meet the challenge. This has been manifested in recurring problems – such as the crisis of migrant workers, unstable incomes and livelihoods for much of the population – that became glaringly visible during the pandemic. The Prime Minister's appeals and assurances from time to time appeared to be inadequate to address the magnitude of the problem. In addition, the strains in Indian democracy were exacerbated during the pandemic period – police violence increased, many democratic elements from the school syllabus were suspended and, overall, government activity was notably opaque (Harriss, 2020; Jha and Pankaj, 2020; Ghosh, 2021).

Corporate Social Responsibility and the pandemic

The pandemic has impacted certain sections of Indian society in disproportionately adverse ways, in many cases well beyond the loss of livelihood or income, up to and including mortality. A problem of such magnitude demanded that companies do more than the perfunctory CSR activities that they engage in during normal times. Social, economic, class, caste and gender inequities have been exacerbated throughout these trying times, and government initiatives such as food, communication and healthcare facilities have failed to bring about a quick remedy when each passing day might mean the difference between life and death for these vulnerable sections of society.

During the First World War, when India was affected by the Spanish flu, the then colonial government displayed inhuman apathy, resulting in millions of deaths. Thankfully, in contrast to the general apathy of the colonial masters and the business entities controlled by them, this time the state and India Inc were empathetic. The corporate entities in particular came forward on their own to help the most adversely affected populations. Several major global companies are also taking wide-scale measures to help respective governments tackle COVID-19. Just as several automakers famously shifted to make tanks and planes during the Second World War, today's corporations are retooling their production lines to make everything from hand sanitizers (LVMH) to respirators (Ford, GE) and ventilators (Dyson). Even if they have been promised readily available markets, such measures nevertheless inspired confidence during these hard times. In India, business houses have unleashed a raft of measures, earning the trust and loyalty of their employees in a marked departure from the onset of the pandemic in 2020 when redundancy and furlough became the new normal. Two years on, many large and small companies are extending financial, medical and educational support to the bereaved family members of their employees who had fallen victim to the pandemic.

Decisions/rules often act as reminders on the applicable subjects – individuals, groups or corporate entity – on what has to be done. In the same vein, the legislation mandating CSR appears to have encouraged massive activism during the pandemic from companies of various scales, from multinational corporations, large national companies to small companies, including start-ups. CSR activism has taken place during various phases, when several crises have surfaced at the same time: one after another 'wave' indicating the pandemic having acquired 'newer' virulence; the migrant labourers' crisis; the acute shortage of oxygen cylinders and other medical facilities; the shortage of vaccines; and above all, serious disruption to normal life, leading to the loss of livelihood and income for the vast majority of people and resulting in abject poverty for so many.

Major global players in business participated in CSR activism. For example, Walmart, Flipkart and the Walmart Foundation announced the provision of Rs 46 crore worth of help that would focus on personal protective equipment, including N95 masks, medical gowns for medical staff and other necessities for vulnerable communities. This process had started with Borosil Limited, the pioneer glassware company in India. It offered two years of salaries to the families of four employees who died of the virus. In addition, the education of the children of these employees would be paid through to graduation.

Reliance Industries Limited, a Fortune 500 listed conglomerate, ramped up production of medical-grade liquid oxygen from near-zero to 1,000 megatonnes per day, which would hopefully meet the needs of over 100,000 critically ill patients per day on average. Sir HN Reliance Foundation Hospital, in collaboration with the Municipal Corporation of Greater Mumbai, set up a dedicated 100-bed centre at Seven Hills Hospital in Mumbai, the nerve-centre of corporate India. Reliance Foundation provided free meals to people across various cities in partnership with nongovernmental organizations during the crisis. Reliance also announced free fuel for all emergency service vehicles in the country (Reliance Foundation, 2021).

Larsen &Toubro's Corporate Technology and Engineering Academy at Mumbai has been converted into a quarantine facility for employees and their family members in Mumbai. The facility is supported by a visiting doctor, full-time nursing staff, ambulance facilities, oxygen concentrator, cylinders, relevant medical equipment, as well as basic medicines. The giant Indian conglomerate with a long history of contribution towards welfare programmes, Tata Steel, has announced social security schemes for the family members of employees affected by the pandemic. Deceased employee's families were to get the last-drawn salary until the superannuation age of 60 years, as well as medical benefits and housing facilities. Their children were assured of financial support until graduation. India's largest bicycle maker Hero Cycles allocated Rs 100 crore as a contingency fund to help the entire ecosystem around the organization to survive the crisis.

Mahindra Group started working on making ventilators for COVID-19 patients. Anand Mahindra, the chairman of the group, also announced that Mahindra Holidays resorts would be offered to the government as temporary care facilities. Besides announcing his decision to donate 100 per cent of his salary to the COVID-19 fund, the chairman also encouraged his colleagues to voluntarily contribute to the fund. Auto major Maruti Suzuki India and the Zydus Group, a prominent pharmaceutical company, started a multi-speciality hospital in Ahmedabad, built with total expenditure funded by the Maruti Suzuki Foundation and converted into a COVID-19 care centre. ITC airlifted 24 cryogenic ISO containers[3] of 20 tonnes each from Asian countries in collaboration with Linde India. ITC also set up three facilities in three states with a total of 600 beds for the treatment of COVID-19 patients.

Even smaller companies and start-ups are offering masks, sanitizers and other essential supplies to prevent shortages in this large country of 1.35 billion people. From making masks and sanitizers to contributing funds, many smaller Indian companies have united to help citizens and the government fight the virus. Diageo India pledged to produce around 300,000 litres of bulk hand sanitizers across 15 of its manufacturing units in the country to help cope with the demand for the product. It also planned to donate 5,00,000 litres of extra neutral alcohol to the sanitizer manufacturing industry to enable the production of more than 2 million units of bottled sanitizers. Diageo India is also planning to support the hospitality sector with Rs 3 crore as health insurance cover for bartenders. As a final example, the Paytm founder, Vijay Shekhar Sharma, has committed Rs 5 crore for the development of medical solutions to fight COVID-19. Worldwide, CSR activism is usually voluntary by nature and the contributions of corporations are not legally enforceable. In India, however, the state's mandate and the pandemic have encouraged the flourishing of CSR activism.

During the pandemic, the poor and destitute in India have had to face many forms of hardship: reports of non-payment and/or underpayment of wages as well as serious exploitation of labour have resurfaced from time to time. At this point, it is necessary to establish procedures of fair trade and fundamental human security. CSR cannot be expected to address issues deeply rooted deeply in economic and political structures, which is beyond its scope. Hence, it is the responsibility of the democratically constituted political authority to address issues that produce poverty, inequality and destitution. CSR activism is at best a second-order supporting factor. Social, economic, class, caste and gender inequities come to the fore in these trying times, and government initiatives have repeatedly failed to bring about a quick remedy when each passing day might mean the difference between life and death for many vulnerable sections of the population. The disheartening picture of the migrant families on their 1,000-kilometre trek from their meagre yet stable sources of daily bread to uncertain yet friendlier homes still haunts our conscience.

When announcing the first phase of lockdown, the Prime Minister sensed severe hardships for the working class, yet instead of clear policy directions, he appealed to the goodwill of people, which proved too little for the subsequent sequence of crises. At the same time, democratic spaces have been constrained significantly and, overall, the government failed to uphold its accountability. In addition, the Prime Minister's Citizen Assistance and Relief in Emergency Situations Fund, created on 27 March 2020, has been subject to severe criticism for its opacity and lack of accountability by disregarding the transparency-provisions from time to time (Ghosh, 2021). Furthermore, we find in Table 5.1 that many companies have pledged or committed sizeable amounts of money for relief.

However, it is not clear how much of that money will be used. At this point, it is necessary to have a democratically constituted authority, where the government and opposition have mutual respect and understanding for a proper direction and realistic use of available funds and resources, and to coordinate programmes in tune with the needs of people. This is possible in a country where the democratic polity is vibrant, marked by political competition and oversight as well as consensus on the core values of human well-being.

Liberal democracy envisages the state to be the 'public actor' that stands over and above various 'private actors', including

Table 5.1: CSR activities of Indian corporates

Sl.	Company Name	CSR Activity
1	Adani Foundation	Contributed Rs 100 crore to PM CARES fund
2	Anita Dogre	Announced 1.5 crore fund to help self-employed artisans
3	Asian Paints	Committed Rs 35 crore to central emergency relief funds
4	Axis Bank	Waived off charges on various bank transactions
5	Bajaj Group	Committed Rs 100 crore
6	Diageo	Donated up to 2 million litres of alcohol to make 8 million bottles of hand-sanitizers
7	Godrej	Initiated Rs 50 crore fund to support and relief works
8	Henkel	Donated to UN and WHO funds and also donated hygiene products
9	Honda	Donated Rs 11 crore aid for preventive measures
10	Hindustan Unilever Limited	Pledged Rs 100 crore price cuts on Lifebuoy and Domex range of products
11	Infosys Foundation	With Narayana Health City, opened a 100-bed quarantine facility
12	ITC (formerly, Imperial Tobacco Company	Created Rs 150 crore contingency fund for helping the marginalized
13	JSW Group	Committed Rs 100 crore to PM CARES fund
14	Larsen &Toubro	Committed Rs 150 crore to PM CARES fund
15	Marico & AT Chandra Foundation	Launched a nationwide hunt for innovative solution with a prize money of Rs 2.5 crore

(continued)

Table 5.1: CSR activities of Indian corporates (continued)

Sl.	Company Name	CSR Activity
16	Ola	Committed Rs 20 crore fund 'Drive the Driver' for its drivers
17	Reliance Industries	Donated Rs 500 crore to PM CARES apart from investing in first COVID hospital in the country
18	State Bank of India	Announced 0.25 per cent of its annual profit to go towards fighting COVID in FY 2020–21
19	Tata Sons	Contributed Rs 1000 crore apart from Rs 500 Crore pledged by various Tata trusts
20	Uday Kotak & Kotak Bank	Committed Rs 60 crore
21	Vedanta	Pledged Rs 100 crore
22	Wipro	Committed Rs 1125 crore for handing the health and humanitarian emergency

CSR activities involved in COVID-19 relief works according to published information on web sources (a random sample, arranged alphabetically):

business, and has the responsibility to promote the overall common good. Even in CSR, business can participate only as a supporting factor (Hussain and Moriarty, 2018: 522–31). In 2020 alone, the rate of unemployment doubled in India, the number of poor people increased by 75 million and the size of the middle class shrank from 99 million to 66 million – all alongside a sharp decline in overall living standards (Das, 2021; Kochhar, 2021). In this context, CSR activism has certainly offered much breathing space during the pandemic, but it has nevertheless proven inadequate compared to the manifold crisis. In fact, it would be unfair to expect CSR, with its limited agenda, to address the deep-rooted structural issues that reproduce poverty and inequality. Providing medical necessities, hospital beds or assisting distressed employees are certainly useful and humane gestures, but we cannot expect much more. For obvious reasons, business and the creation of wealth is the prime goal for the companies concerned; anything else – such as CSR activism – remains secondary. This is not any moral indictment – if business is neglected, the country's economy will be in serious jeopardy.

The ongoing pandemic has led to serious questions being raised about neoliberalism from time to time, on its capacity and intention to generate prosperity with inclusion. Despite this, however, we do not find any practical alternatives to a neoliberal economy. The challenge before the developing world is therefore to negotiate achieving the maximum of common good from the corporate sector. From the Indian experience, several lessons can be learnt: first, firms need to be reminded that they are not above social obligations. As the standard of social responsibility varies from firm to firm, the proactive involvement of the state may help in achieving a common framework of action. Such pro-social engagements, in the long run, are also good for the image of the business. In addition, increased well-being is likely to strengthen their market, as people may like to spend more if their capacity increases. Secondly, when times are not very tough, enacting appropriate laws with the vision of the common good creates the legal infrastructure. Once such rules are formulated, concerned parties can negotiate on that basis and will find it difficult to abdicate them altogether. Finally, CSR is an example. It is not necessary that all developing countries must follow the Indian experiences on CSR legislation uncritically. Rather, it is advisable that the Indian legislation acts as a template – a guide for action. Each country can formulate CSR-like rules to elicit social responsibility from the business sector in accordance with their respective situation and circumstances. The overarching principle should be the state's guidance for the business sector to be socially responsible and contribute to the common good. CSR is a mechanism for corporate firms, large and small, to establish their credentials as responsible and conscientious entities. In India, CSR has to be understood in the context of widespread poverty and destitution: as an instrument for integrating social, environmental and human development concerns in the entire value chain of corporate business. After independence, India embarked on a path of state-led development. Over the course of time, however, private business was gradually able to expand its frontiers in India's socioeconomic milieu, becoming decisive in 1991. Subsequently, the business sector gained a key position in influencing the policymaking process. In 2013, the Indian government made it mandatory for companies to earmark 2 per cent from their net profits for CSR activism. This proved to be quite timely during the COVID-19 pandemic. Many corporate entities of different sizes came forward in many ways and varieties of directions. This proved quite useful. However, CSR activism should not be treated as a panacea for deep-rooted structures that generate socioeconomic inequalities. It is, at best, a second-order supporting factor to the democratically constituted public authority committed to upholding the well-being and existential security of the entire population.

Notes

[1] In fact, this is a potential gain for a company: it is not CSR, but cost-consciousness and environmental awareness might do well for companies in the long run.

[2] There were very few large indigenous private enterprises before independence, such as Tata and Godrej; most were owned by overseas investors.

[3] They are called ISO containers since they are manufactured according to the specifications laid down by the International Organization for Standardization.

References

Agarwal, S.K. (2008) *Corporate Social Responsibility in India*, New Delhi: Response Books.

Corporate Reform Collective (2014) *Fighting Corporate Abuse: Beyond Predatory Capitalism*, London: Pluto.

Das, K. (2021) 'Covid-19: poverty doubled in India in 2020; will second wave make it worse?', *India Today*. Available from: https://www.indiatoday.in/business/story/covid-19-poverty-doubled-in-india-in-2020-will-second-wave-make-it-worse-1793826-2021-04-22

Dun & Bradstreet (2021) 'India's top 500 companies 2020'. Available from: https://www.dnb.co.in/files/pdf/2020/indias-top-500-companies-2020.pdf

Ghosh S. (2021) 'India and the pandemic: democratic governance at crossroads', *International Journal of Asian Studies*, 1–20. Available from: https://doi.org/10.1017/S1479591421000188

Harriss, J. (2020) '"Responding to an epidemic requires a compassionate state": how has the Indian state been doing in the time of COVID-19?', *Journal of Asian Studies*, 79(3): 609–20.

Hussain, W. and Moriarty, J. (2018) 'Accountable to whom? Rethinking the role of corporations in political CSR', *Journal of Business Ethics*, 149:519–34.

Jha, M.K. and Pankaj, A.K. (2020) 'Insecurity and fear travel as labour travels in the time of pandemic', in R. Samaddar (ed), *Borders of an Epidemic: COVID-19 and Migrant Workers*, Kolkata: MCRG, 56–65.

Kaur, R. (2020) *Brand New Nation: Capitalist Dreams and Nationalist Designs in Twenty-First-Century India*, Stanford: Stanford University Press.

Kochhar, R. (2021) 'In the pandemic, India's middle class shrinks and poverty spreads while China sees smaller changes', Pew Research Center. Available from: https://www.pewresearch.org/fact-tank/2021/03/18/in-the-pandemic-indias-middle-class-shrinks-and-poverty-spreads-while-china-sees-smaller-changes

Kohli, A. (2012) *Poverty and Plenty in the New India*, New York: Cambridge University Press.

Ministry of Corporate Affairs (2014) 'The Companies Act 2013'. Available from: https://www.mca.gov.in/content/mca/global/en/acts-rules/ebooks/acts.html?act=NTk2MQ==

Ministry of Corporate Affairs (2020) 'General circular 10/2020'. Available from: https://www.mca.gov.in/Ministry/pdf/Covid_23032020.pdf

Nigam, A. (2002) 'Radical politics in the times of globalization: notes on recent Indian experience', in N.G. Jayal and S. Pai (eds), *Democratic Governance in India: Challenges of Poverty, Development and Identity*, New Delhi: Sage, 153–78.

Reliance Foundation (2021) 'COVID-19 response'. Available from: https://www.reliancefoundation.org/covid-19-response

Rodrik, D. and Subramanian, A. (2004) 'From "Hindu Growth" to productivity surge: the mystery of the Indian growth transition'. Available from: https://www.nber.org/system/files/working_papers/w10376/w10376.pdf

Rowe, J. (2005) 'Corporate social responsibility as business strategy', UC Santa Cruz: Center for Global, International and Regional Studies. Available from: https://escholarship.org/uc/item/5dq43315

Sultana, N. (2020) 'Covid covers 80% of CSR budget for India Inc: CRISIL'. Available from: https://www.livemint.com/companies/news/india-inc-allocated-over-80-of-annual-csr-budget-for-covid-19-crisil-11591715454335.htmlVanaik, A. (1990) *The Painful Transition: Bourgeois Democracy in India*, London: Verso.

SIX

Local Community and Policy Solutions to a Global Pandemic

Pieternella Pieterse

For many hospitals in low- and middle-income countries (LMICs), the global COVID-19 pandemic has meant putting in place preventative measures with limited financial resources and under challenging circumstances. In March and April 2020, personal protective equipment (PPE) was difficult to procure due to shortages caused by a surge in demand, and even harder to import at short notice while commercial flights were grounded (AU, WFP, WHO, 2020).

For the children's cancer ward[1] based at Muhimbili National Hospital in Dar es Salaam, Tanzania, it was no different. As a facility with some international support, it had been able to purchase single-use PPE where needed before the COVID-19 pandemic. However, at the start of the worldwide outbreak, supply lines quickly dried up. In partnership with a local nongovernmental organization (NGO), and with support from the local and international community in Dar es Salaam, it was able to develop a novel solution to protect everyone: locally sourced, reusable PPE was designed and produced for all staff working at the paediatric cancer ward. A strict sterilizing protocol was developed, based on guidance developed during an influenza outbreak a decade earlier (Lore et al, 2012) and rigorously adhered to. Beyond the immediate health benefits, the results of this response are thought to have had positive social, economic and environmental outcomes. They have also had long-lasting positive effects on hospital infection control capabilities that will last well beyond the COVID-19 emergency. These outcomes have the potential to be replicated in other resource-constrained settings.

Producing PPE locally

In March 2020, when the first cases of COVID-19 were officially diagnosed in Tanzania (WHO, 2020), the management of the Children's Cancer Ward decided that everyone, including administrators, cleaners, patients and guardians, would wear a mask at all times regardless of symptoms. The types of masks offered (cloth, surgical or N95) depended on different clinical situations. Outpatients and staff were issued clean cloth masks to wear to and from the hospital. On the ward, everyone wore N95 masks. Children for whom N95 masks were too large were fitted with double masks, a surgical and a cloth mask.

To help meet this need for the additional masks, volunteers from the nearby international school and a local hand-weaving business fundraised and worked with Tanzanian seamstresses to produce over 1,500 cloth masks in two months. The production of other reusable PPE items followed: surgical gowns, scrubs and cap patterns were found online and were sewn by local tailors, who fitted and adjusted them. The material used for the PPE was locally available kitenge, which is tightly woven cotton. The kitenge PPE brought colour to the wards and was well received by staff and patients, who explained that it added to a collective team spirit that replaced the overwhelming sense of fear initially felt by all. The seamstresses involved in the endeavour spoke of feeling proud to support doctors and nurses carrying out important jobs for their community.

The reusable PPE offered many benefits. Costs compared favourably: cloth masks cost 1.30 US$ versus 0.69–5.00 US$ per single-use surgical/N95 mask; cloth gowns cost 5.40

US$ versus 15.00 US$ for disposable options. Reusable products were easier to access, especially in the early months of the pandemic. In addition, their production provided local employment and is more environmentally sustainable. All PPE was cleaned and sterilized daily. Cloth bags were produced, ensuring that every item, clean or dirty, could be stored separately. Safety guidelines outlining use and storage were translated, printed and distributed.

PPE efficacy and its lasting impact

A number of COVID-19 cases were diagnosed among parents and patients on the Children's Cancer Ward. This outbreak was halted rapidly due to the well-rehearsed hygiene protocols and access to sufficient PPE. No staff were known to have contracted the virus. The Children's Cancer Ward management chose a 'mask for all' policy well beyond prevailing international advice, and evidence from the World Health Organization has since validated this decision (WHO, 2020). The team gained confidence in the protective measures and pride in overcoming this difficult time together. In the context of a large government hospital, where wages cannot always be supplemented even when a specialist wing receives external funding, the explicit focus on the safety of staff and their families, as well as the patients, improved staff morale and dedication to their jobs during a challenging period.

The full PPE kits were in daily use for around eight months, until it became clear that patients and staff could be protected from the virus by focusing primarily on mask wearing, as well as handwashing and the retention of certain additional cleaning routines. Similar improved hygiene protocols are thought to have been instituted in many healthcare facilities across Tanzania, which is a welcome development given the findings from a pre-COVID-19 study, which noted that low adherence to cleaning and hand hygiene protocols were the norm. A study focusing on the COVID-19 responses of local health officials in Tanzania showed that officials in four locations interviewed in July 2020 highlighted a range of coping strategies that were employed at local level, often in the absence of national-level guidance, including the production of locally made face masks and hand sanitizer and greater efforts of local health authorities to make water for handwashing available in health facilities (Carlitz et al, 2021).

COVID-19 politicized

The use of locally produced PPE at the children's cancer ward and at other locations served as a sustainable solution as well as a culturally and politically acceptable way of keeping patients and staff safe. In April 2020, the approach taken in response to COVID-19 by Tanzania's then President started to diverge widely from that of heads of state regionally and internationally (Nakkazi, 2020), which politicized any measures taken to protect people from the virus. To those who followed the individual COVID-19 responses of LMICs, it was clear relatively early on in the pandemic that Tanzania had adopted an unorthodox way of dealing with the virus. The first case of COVID-19 infection in Tanzania was confirmed on 16 March, and like many other countries in the region, a series of transmission reduction orders were announced. On 17 March 2020, Prime Minister Kassim Majaliwa announced the initial measures to control local COVID-19 transmission: closure of all school levels and a ban on all public or social gatherings (Makoni, 2021).

On 23 March, the government declared that all incoming travellers from COVID-19-affected countries would be quarantined for two weeks at their own cost (APO Group, 2020). While the countries surrounding Tanzania suspended all public worship in churches, mosques and other religious institutions, President John Magufuli declared that COVID-19 was "the work of the devil and public worship in churches and mosques should continue because prayer can defeat coronavirus disease" (Nakkazi, 2020). On 10 April, when reported cases of COVID-19 infections had reached over 750 and it was clear there was widespread community infection, President Magufuli asked Tanzanian citizens to pray for three days in their respective churches and mosques to seek protection from God against the disease.

In May 2020, the President declared Tanzania COVID free and suspended the release of all test results. It was not until the President himself passed away in March of the following year that any test results were officially released (although it is thought that tests were carried out on an individual basis without central authorities being informed). It was perhaps not surprising that in February 2021, when donations of COVID-19 vaccines became available through the COVAX initiative, they were turned down by the Tanzanian government. "We are not yet satisfied that those vaccines have been clinically proven safe", Health Minister Dorothy Gwajima was quoted as saying during a news conference. Gwajima went on to warn journalists about reporting unofficial figures on COVID-19 or any disease (Makoni, 2021: 566). In an interview with the BBC, the government's chief spokesperson Hassan Abbas cited concerns about the brief suspension of the Oxford–AstraZeneca vaccine in South Africa, among other reasons. In the meantime, ministers and other officials often went about their daily duties, especially those visible to the public, unmasked (Makoni, 2021: 566). The pressure to affirm the President's views and policies was noticeable in the media (Mwangale Kiptinness and Okoye, 2021), and in peer-reviewed journal contributions by Tanzanian scholars and medics (Buguzi, 2021), which was hardly surprising given the large fines and shutdowns that were meted out against any broadcaster judged in breach of Tanzania's new media and cybercrime laws (Amnesty International, 2020).

COVID-19 deaths

Within the first 12 months of the COVID-19 pandemic, Tanzania lost a significant number of high-level officials, including former President Benjamin Mkapa, Foreign Minister Augustine Mahiga and Zanzibar's First Vice-President and national chairman of the opposition ACT-Wazalendo Party Seif Sharif Hamad (The Citizen, 2020), as well as many other leading politicians, academics and businesspeople. Of those mentioned, only Seif Sharaf Hamad's death was publicly attributed to COVID-19, though rumours about the causes of death of the other dignitaries were hard to suppress. In March 2021, President Magufuli died. He had not been seen or heard in public for a week, and the country appeared at a loss as to how to react (BBC, 2021). The official line was that he died because of 'heart complications', which many believe were exacerbated by COVID-19 (Cheeseman et al, 2021).

The death of President Magufuli brought about many changes, including a change in policy in relation to COVID-19. Tanzania's new president, Samia Suluhu Hassan – who had been vice-president during President Magufuli's time in office – stated publicly in April 2021 that it is "not proper to ignore" the COVID-19 pandemic (Al Jazeera, 3 April 2021). In July 2021, the first consignment of COVID-19 vaccines arrived in Tanzania, which were delivered through the COVAX facility (WHO, 2021).

Tanzania's comparative health performance in Eastern and Southern Africa

Given that the rate of vaccination in most LMICs remains extremely low, Tanzania's late start in terms of vaccination uptake has therefore not put it significantly behind some of its Eastern and Southern African neighbours, despite its unorthodox approach in the first 12 months of the pandemic. In December 2021, Tanzania's neighbouring countries were reported to have achieved the following full vaccination rates: Rwanda 30 per cent, Kenya 6 per cent, Zambia 4.5 per cent, Malawi 3.3 per cent, Uganda 2.8 per cent, Ethiopia 1.3 per cent and Burundi close to nil – around 500 people fully vaccinated (Mathieu et al, 2021). Going into 2022, Tanzania's vaccination rate amounted to three doses received per 100 people, with an unknown number of individuals fully vaccinated.[2]

Tanzania can be found below Kenya, Rwanda and Uganda on the Human Development Report but above Malawi, Ethiopia and the Democratic Republic of the Congo (UNDP, 2020). In terms of the infant mortality rate, Tanzania performs better than Mozambique and Zambia but lags behind neighbours Malawi, Rwanda and Kenya (UNICEF, 2021). Tanzania's decentralized health system has suffered from years of underfunding: '[C]urrent public spending on health is insufficient to provide access to quality services to all', according to a public expenditure review published in 2020, which noted a decline in healthcare expenditure as a share of GDP, which amounted to only 6 per cent in 2017 (World Bank, 2020). The hope among many in Tanzania is that the new leadership may bring renewed interest in improved healthcare provision in a wider sense. With Tanzania's current engagement in the receipt and distribution of COVID-19 vaccines, it is anticipated that it, along with many other poorly provisioned LMICs, will soon be able to obtain more equitable access to much needed COVID-19 vaccines.

Local responses to COVID-19

Although it is important to highlight the unusual response from Tanzania's former leader to the challenges of the COVID-19 pandemic, which determined the headlines at a global and national level, it is important to emphasize that evidence is slowly emerging of many localized responses to the virus that were careful, well thought out, used local resources as much as possible and often adhered to international best practice. A 'letter to the editor' written by two medics associated with two hospitals and teaching facilities, submitted to an international medical journal in September 2020, serves to remind people that Tanzania's public health promotion campaigns, which were focusing on education and training to raise awareness of COVID-19 transmission and prevention, continued to be heeded by many, long after the risk of infection had apparently been banished, at least according to the country's leaders. A paper published by physicians at one of Dar es Salaam's best-known private health facilities, the Aga Khan Hospital, highlights that in the early months of the COVID-19 pandemic, their uptake of telemedicine increased significantly, indicating that among the better off, coping strategies were adopted that were similar to those in the Global North (Ortega et al, 2020). The research conducted by Carlitz et al (2021) likewise shows that at local level, health officials, healthcare staff and ordinary citizens took action in a variety of ways to protect themselves and their fellow citizens from the possible threat of COVID-19: 'Several district-level officers reported local manufacturing of hand sanitizers and face masks. Ward-level officers were the ones primarily charged with educating their communities and ensuring compliance with mask wearing and hand washing' (Carlitz et al, 2021: 1005). Much like turning to reusable PEE made from locally available materials in one Dar es Salaam hospital, Tanzanians country-wide appear to have responded to the challenges that COVID-19 brought with a resourcefulness that has probably served them well in the past decade of having to cope with an underfunded health service. When unexpected events happen, individuals and communities often respond to shocks with ingenuity, even when political constraints further influence the range of coping mechanisms that can be employed. Lessons for the wider international community include ensuring that local-level responses are supported where possible, not overlooked. It is also important that external forces, aid donors, charities and others make efforts to understand political contexts in order to be able to provide suitable responses and be sympathetic to the real or perceived threats that may be experienced by those in need of support.

Overall, evidence is emerging that Tanzanians' responses to the COVID-19 pandemic may have been influenced by a leadership that acted in ways that were highly unusual, undermining the health of many thousands of citizens. At the same time, it also appears that many Tanzanian citizens acted in ways that were sensible, wise and motivated by care and concern for their families, communities and themselves. In wider debates about vaccine inequity and the threats that large unvaccinated populations cause to the whole world, it is important to understand how each individual country arrived at their current position in order to determine how best to support and stand in solidarity with the citizens of individual nations.

Notes

[1] The paediatric oncology ward at Muhimbili University Hospital is managed by a mix of charity-funded and public hospital staff. The charity Tumaini La Maisha provides free cancer treatment and holistic care to all paediatric oncology patients at Muhimbili and a network of 11 associated hospitals and healthcare facilities throughout Tanzania. https://www.wearetlm.org/our-story-in-detail

[2] See https://covidvax.live/location/tza

References

Al Jazeera (2021) 'Tanzania's new president says it's "not proper" to ignore COVID', 3 April. Available from: https://www.aljazeera.com/news/2021/4/6/tanzanias-new-president-says-not-proper-to-ignore-covid

Amnesty International (2020) 'Tanzania 2020'. Available from: https://www.amnesty.org/en/location/africa/east-africa-the-horn-and-great-lakes/tanzania/report-tanzania

APO Group (2020) 'Coronavirus – Tanzania: travel advisory no. 1 of 23.03.2020 – update on COVID-19 in Tanzania, 2020'. Available from: https://www.africa-newsroom.com/press/coronavirus--tanzania-travel-advisory-no1-of-23032020-update-on-covid19-in-tanzania?lang=en

AU, WFP, WHO (2020) 'First UN solidarity flight departs Addis Ababa carrying vital COVID-19 medical supplies to all African nations', 14 April. Available from: https://www.who.int/news-room/det ail/14-04-2020-first-un-solidarity-flight-departs-addis-ababa-carry ing-vital-covid-19-medical-supplies-to-all-african-nations

BBC (2021) 'John Magufuli: Tanzania's president dies aged 61 after Covid rumours', 18 February. Available from: https://www.bbc. com/news/world-africa-56437852

Buguzi, S. (2021) 'Covid-19: counting the cost of denial in Tanzania', *British Medical Journal*, 373.

Carlitz, R., Yamanis, T. and Mollel, H. (2021) 'Coping with denialism: how street-level bureaucrats adapted and responded to COVID-19 in Tanzania', *Journal of Health Politics, Policy and Law*, 46(6): 989–1017.

Cheeseman, N., Matfess, H. and Amani, A. (2021) 'Tanzania: the roots of repression', *Journal of Democracy*, 32(2): 77–89.

The Citizen (2020) 'Death robs Tanzania of 10 prominent persons in February', 23 February. Available from: https://www.theeast african.co.ke/tea/news/east-africa/-death-robs-tanzania-of-10-prominent-persons-in-february-3301530

COVIDVAX.LIVE (2022) 'Live COVID-19 vaccination tracker'. Available from: https://covidvax.live/location/tza

Lore, M.B., Heimbuch, B.K., Brown, T.L., Wander, J.D. and Hinrichs, S.H. (2012) 'Effectiveness of three decontamination treatments against influenza virus applied to filtering facepiece respirators', *Ann. Occup. Hyg.*, 56(1): 92–101.

Makoni, M. (2021) 'Tanzania refuses COVID-19 vaccines', *The Lancet*, 397(10274): 566.

Mathieu, E., Roser, M., Hasell, J. and Appel, C. (2021) 'A global database of COVID-19 vaccinations', *Nat. Hum. Behav.* Available from: https://ourworldindata.org/covid-vaccinations?country= OWID_WRL

Mwangale Kiptinness, E. and Okoye, J.B. (2021) 'Media coverage of the novel Coronavirus (Covid-19) in Kenya and Tanzania: content analysis of newspaper articles in East Africa', *Cogent Medicine*, 8(1): 1956034.

Nakkazi, E. (2020) 'Obstacles to COVID-19 control in East Africa', *The Lancet. Infectious Diseases*, 20(6): 660.

Ortega, G., Rodriguez, J.A., Maurer, L.R., Witt, E.E., Perez, N., Reich, A. et al (2020) 'Telemedicine, COVID-19, and disparities: policy implications', *Health Policy and Technology*, 9(3): 368–71.

UNDP (2020) 'Human Development Index 2020', New York: UNDP.

UNICEF (2021) 'The state of the world's children 2021'. Available from: https://data.unicef.org/resources/sowc-2021-dashboard-and-tables

World Bank (2020) 'Tanzania public expenditure review 2020', Washington.

WHO (2020) 'Advice on the use of masks in the context of COVID-19', 5 June. Available from: https://www.who.int/emergencies/diseases/novel-coronavirus-2019/advice-for-pub lic/when-and-how-to-use-masks

WHO (2021) 'The United Republic of Tanzania receives the first COVAX shipment', 24 July. Available from: https://www.afro. who.int/news/united-republic-tanzania-receives-first-covax-shipment

SEVEN

Pandemic Structure and Blowback: Endemic Inequality and the New (ab)Normal

Pádraig Carmody and Gerard McCann

Neoliberal theorists, such as Milton Friedman (1970), argue that greed and inequality are good. They incentivize people to become entrepreneurs, while a high capital share in total income encourages investment and innovation. This position remains at the core of International Monetary Fund (IMF) programmes, which increased global inequality (Lensink, 1996). There is some truth to these arguments, perhaps, but untrammelled inequality also has massive social costs, particularly in a pandemic when vaccine inequity is evident, pervasive, socially and individually destructive – neoliberal protestations about the rights of the latter notwithstanding. The culture and practice of greed and inequality has followed us through to the pandemic. Wealth and vaccine hoarding in rich countries allow for new, potentially more dangerous variants of COVID-19 to develop in parts of the Global South. As Ngcobo and Pogge have argued in this volume, this is functional, in particular, for global pharmaceutical corporations, as it provides a temporally unlimited, if spatially and socially limited market, which co-constitute as described below, allowing endless accumulation of capital. However, there are massive costs in terms of public health, both in the Global North and South, deadweight losses for economies as a result of COVID-19 restrictions and wasted public expenditure. This comes with huge opportunity costs in terms of social investment, green transitions and infrastructural adaptation, among other things. Critically, vaccine nationalism in the Global North has resulted in 'blowback' or unintended consequences of policy actions that boomerang on their architects (Johnson, 2002). However, it is blowback with distinctive characteristics, as it appears to be setting off a cycle of revaccination (for some), mutation and repetition, although in time the virus may become endemic.

The current pandemic structure has allowed the virus to mutate and develop new variants, some of which seem to have engaged in, or are close to, vaccine escape (such as Omicron). While the desire of governments in the Global North to protect their own populations is understandable and necessary, it does not conform even to the logic of 'enlightened self-interest', which would suggest simultaneous global vaccination roll-out. Indeed, the outcomes of COVID-19 could be viewed through the lens of the biopolitical imperative (Foucault and Senellart, 2008), where one of the main priorities of governments in rich countries is the protection and 'flourishing' of life, while many living in the Global South are condemned to sacrificial 'bare life' (Agamben, 2005).

The pandemic cycle and structure

As a global society, we seem to be caught in a pandemic cycle that is structured, reproduced and reinforced by prevailing patterns of power and politics, which mostly emphasize national over international responsibilities. Some populist governments, such as Boris Johnson's Conservative administration in the UK, initially won plaudits for their handling of the pandemic through a focus on their national (monopolizing) vaccination programmes. However, as national experiences and responses unfold, the emerging pandemic structure has put paid to the idea that vaccine nationalism can work as an effective strategy to defeat it.

The pandemic sociospatial structure is reflective of broader social processes, structures and policies. Those promoting the latest phase of neoliberalism, defined more openly as libertarianism in many circles in recent years (from the Tea Party movement in the United States to the Brexiteer Conservatives of the UK), show little interest in the sweeping impact of global issues, favouring instead 'radical supply side reform'. Indeed, bar conflict (and the 2022 Ukraine war has been an example), there has been a general withdrawal from partnership-based development, certainly from the onset of the 'Great Recession'. The economic nationalism that has accompanied the recent policy preference in some countries of the Global North for market-focused disruptive innovation is nothing new in economics, but it is particularly problematic during crises – such as the pandemic – as it accentuates and compounds gross economic and social inequality internally and globally. The process has been marked by the growth of public food banks, homelessness and destitution, the withdrawal of overseas aid for low-income countries (LICs) (Loft and Brien, 2021: 8), the deliberate neglect of not-for-profit healthcare, the redirection of public funding into politically favoured sectors, tax avoidance and the disregard of the rights of vulnerable migrants on a scale not seen since the Second World War. Ultimately, it leaves highly exposed communities and sectors open to the spread of the virus and the unmitigated circumstances of hardship.

There has often been high-level disregard of the social impact of market liberalization and associated economic inequalities that emanate from the ideological outworking of neoliberalism. Indeed, in some ways circumspection is its purpose. In the first phase of neoliberalism, it was about the consolidation of influence and power acquisition to revive profits. In this latter phase, applied on a global plane, it has been partly about the targeting and the acquisition of public resources and finances through the most predatory inculcation of a rapidly shifting and volatile market system. The pandemic provided a perfect platform for such market adjustment, most visibly evident with the surge of opportunities for the pharmaceutical industries and medical supplies. The scramble for contracts regarding the provision of personal protective equipment (PPE) at the beginning of the pandemic was symptomatic of this model of market expansion. In the UK alone, in one of the biggest public spending sprees ever, the equivalent of $22 billion was disbursed, with an estimated $11 billion going to friends and family of the governing Conservative Party in a so-call 'VIP-Lane'; $5 billion went to politically connected companies that had histories of fraud or tax evasion (*The New York Times*, 17 December 2020). The UK's Test and Trace system cost £37 billion despite being ineffective in monitoring the spread of the virus (House of Commons, 2021: 3). In other countries, the audit of this market anarchy is ongoing.

While public healthcare systems across the world struggled to cope with the scale of COVID-19 patient admissions to hospitals, with supplies of PPE and remediation/oxygen to deal with respiratory collapse becoming ever more scarce, the draw on public resources for vaccine production was staggering. In a stakeholder briefing from late 2021 – almost two years after the start of the pandemic – Oxfam revealed the levels of the profiteering and the strategic targeting of markets by certain pharmaceutical companies to the disregard of global health issues or growing levels of inequality:

Pfizer, BioNTech and Moderna – are making combined profits of $65,000 every minute ... These companies have sold the majority of doses to rich countries, leaving low-income countries out in the cold. Pfizer and BioNTech have delivered less than one percent of their total vaccine supplies to low-income countries, while Moderna has delivered just 0.2 percent. Meanwhile 98 percent of people in low income countries have not been fully vaccinated. (Oxfam, 2021)

During the initial crisis, vaccine development was heavily state-subsidized, and procurement and profits were negotiated behind closed doors, with open tenders suspended and bespoke contacts being agreed at totally unjustifiable profit margins. Rational financial decision-making was decoupled from international protocol as automatic financial stabilizers were disregarded out of fear of a pandemic-related economic shock. Global macroeconomics have, to an extent, adapted through a pandemic economy, as a network of competitive pharmaceuticals (for example, PPE suppliers, vaccine producers, track and trace companies, among others) have emerged as major global market drivers.

Neoliberalism, by its very nature, sources profits habitually. Those who engage in its development seek opportunity in adversity (Klein, 2008), and accelerating economic disparities are a component of this model of development. The pandemic has brought this method of economic 'rebalancing' into the health sector in a vicious manner, where millions of lives were put at risk globally at the behest of market competition between transnational corporations and the opening up by susceptible governments of public finances. In terms of neoliberalism as a method of economic 'advancement', the pandemic has been one of the most exceptional opportunities in human history, as demonstrated by sky-rocketing income inequality and a ballooning number of billionaires globally. Forbes reported 500 new billionaires in the first year of the pandemic, with 61 in healthcare alone. Such inequality, however, provokes the question of economic justice and ways beyond this systemically divisive and damaging way of doing economics – also known as financialization.

The financialization of health

There are a variety of definitions of what constitutes financialization. For some, it is when most of the profits in an economy are financial rather than arising out of production or trade, for example. Epstein defines financialization as 'the increasing role of financial motives, financial markets, financial actors, and financial institutions in the operation of the domestic and international economies' (2005: 3). Financialization has been driven by what some in the financial community call 'economic value added', which does not refer to the amount of value added to a product, for example, but rather the profit that any economic activity can yield, irrespective of its contribution or detriment to the real economy, such as through currency speculation (Coe and Yeung, 2015). With record low interest rates after the global financial crisis (GFC), money capital on deposit effectively ceased being capital for ordinary people and instead became a 'pure' resource for the financial sector to invest – contributing to both inequality and recursively to further financialization. The counter-intuitive deepening of financialization after the GFC fuelled inequality and contributed to the emerging pandemic structure:

> Debt within capitalist modernity is a social technology of power ... In capitalism, the prevailing logic is the logic of differential accumulation, and given that debt instruments far outweigh equity instruments, we can safely claim that interest-bearing debt is the primary way in which economic inequality is generated as more money is redistributed to creditors. (Di Muzio and Robbins, 2016: 7)

As a logic and as described above, financialization has come to structure healthcare delivery in many places around the world and global public health. So influential has the financial sector become in terms of its ability to discipline governments and productive businesses that some speak of 'financial socialism', where there was unprecedented public support for the sector in the wake of the GFC (Woodley, 2019).

According to neoliberal logic, super-profits (substantially above the average rate of profit) are necessary to incentivize innovation. This follows the logic of differential accumulation and financialization, where equity investors buy shares in the most profitable companies, such as global patented monopoly pharma, to maximize dividends. However, this financialized logic comes into direct contradiction with public health in the case of the pandemic and does not necessarily even serve the interests of shareholders in these companies, who also live under the threat of illness and potential death as a result of the ongoing, adaptive and recursive nature of the pandemic. This creates a pandemic structure shaped and undergirded by global inequality, which the pandemic itself seems to be reproducing in cruel and unforeseen ways.

Breaking the cycle

Inequality contributes to vaccine inequity, which is also structured by financial imperatives around 'shareholder value', again contributing to a vicious cycle. Uneven exposure to COVID-19 further deepens inequality, concentrates capital and repeats the cycle in combination with other drivers. COVID-19 inequality is not only raced, classed and gendered but also structured along other axes of identity and positionality. We were able to recognize the multifaceted nature of the inequity very quickly in this pandemic. The impact of the pandemic along with often disjointed governmental responses revealed the disproportionate effect it was having on the poorest sections of society: low-paid workers, those in public care settings, service sectors – those who were in some instances defined as 'essential workers', migrants and those with little or no healthcare cover. As the World Health Organization interpreted it, politically driven responses 'globally' have had devastating effects in regions where poverty and income inequality are highest:

There is increasing evidence that the unequal impact of COVID-19 and its containment measures on different groups in the population was neither fully anticipated nor well considered in the design and implementation of government response plans ... Protecting the most vulnerable is a political choice: measures taken now can mitigate the negative social and economic impacts of COVID-19 on health equity. The socioeconomic profile and trajectory of recovery depends on the willingness and ability of countries to invest early and throughout their recovery and transition phases in equity-sensitive public policies and in their health systems. (WHO, 2021: 1; 13)

Several interventions have emanated from organizations taking global leadership in the delivery of a coordinated recovery that are worth highlighting in the third year of this pandemic. For instance, writing for the IMF, Joseph Stiglitz (2020) insisted that the pandemic would not be over until it has been controlled globally and the rules of economic development rewritten. He argues for mitigations taken through health policy actions as well as socioeconomic initiatives that would combat anticipated economic shocks, particularly debt crises (see Zajontz, 2021), that run parallel to the health crisis. For Stiglitz, there is the option to reset the very functionality of the global economy, for the developed economies – even from the mindset of self-preservation – to move to end global inequalities through assistance and development in its broadest sense. The objective here is convergence, although this of course runs up in reality against the law of combined and uneven development. Perhaps the realistic aim should be levelling up as a process, and a reduction in intercountry inequality, rather than absolute convergence.

Also flagged up was the Group of 20's role and their ability to influence the IMF to create Special Drawing Rights (SDRs) for LICs, which happened to a limited extent in August 2021. This would create financial stability that could help more vulnerable economies spend through the storm, particularly by investing in public services. It was a means used to address the fallout of the GFC in 2009 and remains one mechanism for recovery, if, and crucially, the most developed countries have the (self-)understanding to deliver on this:

> The provision of SDRs would be of enormous assistance to developing economies and emerging markets – with no or little cost to the taxpayers of developed economies. It would be even better if those economies contributed their SDRs to a trust fund to be used by developing economies to meet the exigencies of the pandemic. (Stiglitz, 2020: 19–20)

Beyond that, there is also a network of UN initiatives aimed at post-pandemic recovery. Working through the fog of political fear, fiscal and monetary policies that directly respond to the stressed aspects of economic development has the potential to adapt global financial structures in a manner that can be positively regenerative. It would mean direct and targeted support for households, healthcare for all, protection from unemployment, social protection in its broadest sense, and supporting businesses (particularly indigenous firms) from insolvency.

As early as 20 March 2020, António Guterres, the Secretary-General of the UN, saw this pandemic as decisive in the history of international development. In his report titled 'The recovery from the COVID-19 crisis must lead to a different economy', he led an early engagement with the issues of post-pandemic economic models. While lauded in the Global South, the approach was given less of a hearing in the Global North:

> What is needed is a large-scale, coordinated and comprehensive multilateral response amounting to at least 10 per cent of global GDP [gross domestic product] ... But we must massively increase the resources available to the developing world ... to rapidly inject resources into the countries that need them. Coordinated swaps among central banks can also bring liquidity to emerging

economies. Debt alleviation must be a priority – including immediate waivers on interest payments. (Guterres, 2020)

Harnessing the resources of the UN, the organization also announced their Trust Fund for COVID-19 Response and Recovery, which had the objective of supporting low- and middle-income countries in building up the capacity to not only mitigate the worst effects of the virus but also to take on the formidable task of recovery. Crucially, the strategy that was started over two years ago envisaged future defences against new variants and pandemics, building for economic resilience, confronting climate change as a contextual environment, and addressing systemic inequalities. That said, into the third year and with the continued widespread political preference for COVID nationalism (and blowback), the ideal of 'leaving no one behind' in the recovery remains highly aspirational.

What is becoming ever more apparent is that coordinated and resourced international action combining the capacities and resources of state, market and civil society actors is required to bring the pandemic under control. There is also a palpable need for solidarity of purpose regarding such a threat to humanity on a global scale. The only way to break the current pandemic structure would appear to be through global consciousness and the treatment of vaccines as global public goods – as non-profit, which should be distributed on the basis of need rather than ability to pay. The infusion of the neoliberal logic of profit maximization into global health has resulted in the current catastrophe and conundrum. Part of the answer to this problem must be the (partial) decommodification of health. This approach will, however, likely be strongly resisted by transnational pharmaceutical companies, which might argue that it would interfere with incentives to develop adapted vaccines that respond to new variants.

Accountability in the global economic system provides one answer to pandemic mitigation and the disciplining and regulation of sectors (particularly pharmaceutical and medical) crucial to human development in its broadest of senses. This should include government-facilitated sharing of intellectual property and know-how for the global production of vaccines and COVID-19-related medication. The corollary of this is that global recovery in practice has to be an act of solidarity in order to be fully effective. Indeed, governments will need to work together to ensure coherence in recovery, and a process of developing out of the pandemic together:

> The pandemic won't be controlled until it is controlled everywhere, and the economic downturn won't be tamed until there is a robust global recovery. That's why it's a matter of self-interest – as well as a humanitarian concern – for the developed economies to provide the assistance the developing economies and emerging markets need. Without it, the global pandemic will persist longer than it otherwise would, global inequalities will grow, and there will be global divergence. (Stiglitz, 2021)

The defeat of this pandemic and the prevention of future ones will require a reduction in vaccine and other forms of inequality. This will in turn require a rupture from the dominant logics of financialization. However, financialization's mutability, fungibility and structural power make this a difficult task requiring something akin to a new Bretton Woods Agreement. Pandemic incentives may in time illuminate this alternative and imperative to prevent further societal blowback.

References

Agamben, G. (2005) *State of Exception*, Chicago: University of Chicago Press.

Coe, N.M. and Yeung, H.W.C. (2015) *Global Production Networks: Theorizing Economic Development in an Interconnected World* (1st edn), Oxford: Oxford University Press.

Di Muzio, T. and Robbins, R.H. (2016) *Debt as Power*, Manchester: Manchester University Press.

Epstein, G.A. (2005) *Financialisation and the World Economy*, Cheltenham: Edward Elgar.

Foucault, M. and Senellart, M. (2008) *The Birth of Biopolitics: Lectures at the College de France, 1978–79*, Basingstoke: Palgrave Macmillan.

Friedman, M. (1970) 'The social responsibility of business is to increase its profits', *The New York Times*, 13 September. Available from: https://www.nytimes.com/1970/09/13/archives/a-friedman-doctrine-the-social-responsibility-of-business-is-to.html

Guterres, A, (2020) 'The recovery from the COVID-19 crisis must lead to a different economy', United Nations COVID-19 Response, 20 March. Available from: https://www.un.org/en/un-coronavirus-communications-team/launch-report-socio-economic-impacts-covid-19

House of Commons (2021) 'Test and trace update', Committee of Public Accounts, 21 October. Available from: https://committees.parliament.uk/publications/7651/documents/79945/default

Johnson, C. (2002) *Blowback: The Costs and Consequences of American Empire*, London: Sphere Books.

Klein, N. (2008) *Shock Doctrine: The Rise of Disaster Capitalism*, London: Penguin.

Lensink, R. (1996) *Structural Adjustment in Sub-Saharan Africa*, London: Longman.

Loft, P. and Brien, P. (2021) 'Reducing the UK's aid spending in 2021', London: House of Commons Library, 5 November. Available from: https://researchbriefings.files.parliament.uk/documents/CBP-9224/CBP-9224.pdf

The New York Times (2020) 'Waste, negligence and cronyism: inside Britain's pandemic spending', 17 December. Available from: https://www.nytimes.com/interactive/2020/12/17/world/europe/britain-covid-contracts.html

Oxfam (2021) 'Pfizer, BioNTech and Moderna making $1,000 profit every second while world's poorest countries remain largely unvaccinated', 16 November. Available from: https://www.oxfam. org/en/press-releases/pfizer-biontech-and-moderna-making-1000-profit-every-second-while-worlds-poorest

Stiglitz, J. (2020) 'Conquering the great divide', IMF F&D. Available from: https://www.imf.org/external/pubs/ft/fandd/2020/09/COVID19-and-global-inequality-joseph-stiglitz.htm

Stiglitz, J. (2021) 'Nobel laureate Joseph Stiglitz on how to fix the economy during and after the pandemic', VOX. Available from: https://www.vox.com/covid-19-coronavirus-economy-recession-stock-market/21536710/joseph-stiglitz-interview-covid-19-recovery

WHO (2021) 'Health inequity and the effects of COVID-19'. Available from: https://apps.who.int/iris/bitstream/handle/10665/338199/WHO-EURO-2020-1744-41495-56594-eng.pdf

Woodley, D. (2019) *Finance, Accumulation and Monetary Power: Understanding Financial Socialism in Advanced Capitalist Economies*, London: Routledge.

Zajontz, T. (2021) 'Debt, distress, dispossession: towards a critical political economy of Africa's financial dependency', *Review of African Political Economy*, 49(71):173–83.

EIGHT

Ending a Pandemic

Zeke Ngcobo and Thomas Pogge

"The business of business is business" proclaimed Milton Friedman, one of the most famous economists of the 20th century. This catchy phrase implicitly makes three key points. Firms ought to be focused on promoting shareholder interest, on making profit, the more the better – but they should do this, one might add, without blatant violation of the law (grey zones are another matter). Moreover, governments, regulators and the general public ought to let firms get on with this job: they should keep legal restraints and regulatory burdens slight and simple so that firms can go about their business with minimal constraints, distractions and friction costs. Finally, firms and economists should prod and lobby officials and the public towards the right – light – approach that gives firms the freedom to prosper.

Friedman's view is widely shared among people in the business world, in the financial sector, in economics departments, in politics and the general public. It resonates with the idea that freedom is good in itself. It also draws support from the thought, powerfully articulated by Bernard Mandeville (1714) and Adam Smith (1776), that the profit motive is a stronger, more reliable source of public benefit than altruistic virtue.

Imagine a pharmaceutical sector that takes Friedman's mantra to heart, firms that exist in the world as we know it, dependent upon monopoly markups for their earnings and single-mindedly devoted to advancing shareholder interest. How would such – hypothetical – companies respond to something like the COVID-19 outbreak? Such firms would want to get one or more suitable pharmaceuticals on to the market quickly and then sell such products as profitably as possible, where profit depends on the sales volume and the size of the markup (the unit price minus variable cost of production). Accordingly, such Friedmanian firms would want relevant pharmaceuticals to be in high demand, as measured by the amount of money that solvent buyers are willing to spend, and they would want to appropriate as much of these potential earnings as possible.

High market demand is driven by need. The need generated by the outbreak of a new disease is greater the more harmful the disease and the more widely it spreads. If the outbreak becomes a pandemic, then many more people will be and feel at risk – and at greater risk of exposure and infection. Need is increased also when such a pandemic lasts longer and especially when it evolves dangerous new variants that, by requiring additional innovations, open new research and development (R&D) challenges with new profit opportunities.

Even if buyers would be prepared to pay a very high price for a product, they will naturally try to obtain it for much less. They will succeed if the market is well supplied by competing sellers. A Friedmanian firm will therefore want to impede competition and limit supply in order to induce anxious buyers to pay higher prices.

Confronted with an infectious disease outbreak, the general public has three key interests:

1. That innovators quickly develop or identify pharmaceuticals that can effectively protect individuals from harm and help contain and suppress the disease at the population level.
2. That production of such effective pharmaceuticals be rapidly scaled up to meet the global need.

3. That supply, as it becomes available, be directed to where it can avert the most harm, taking population effects into account.

How well would Friedmanian firms operating under a monopoly patent regime serve these interests? Such firms would want:

1. To quickly develop new pharmaceuticals that can effectively protect individuals from harm *without* impeding the proliferation of the disease.
2. To scale up production of such new pharmaceuticals judiciously in order to capture market share even while safeguarding proprietary technologies and know-how, avoiding wasteful excess capacity and maintaining a favourable demand–supply imbalance to sustain high prices.
3. To prioritize buyers who are offering to pay more and to reject potential buyers who, only marginally profitable, might erode the product price and are more useful spreading and prolonging the epidemic with the potential emergence of new disease variants.
4. To forestall regulatory interference in – and public awareness of – their profit-maximizing stratagems by making it appear that fighting the disease as effectively as possible is really their most profitable strategy or, more plausibly, that they are wholeheartedly dedicated to this fight, profits be damned.

While actual pharmaceutical firms are not motivated by profit alone, they are nevertheless motivated by profit. Profit is what large shareholders – hedge funds and other professional investors – care greatly about; and such shareholders have the power to reward, to discipline and even to fire non-compliant CEOs and are forever breathing down their necks. It should not be too surprising, then, that, on closer inspection, our experience with the COVID-19 pandemic is uncomfortably close to what would have happened in a world of exclusively profit-maximizing firms.

The COVID-19 pandemic

COVID-19 has infected a substantial percentage of humanity. Despite billions of vaccine doses delivered to nearly all countries and territories worldwide, millions of people have either succumbed to the virus or been left with debilitating long-term ailments (UNICEF, 2022). The global surge in numbers affected by this pandemic has triggered R&D into an effective vaccine in record time – under one year as against the previous record of four years achieved in the development of the mumps vaccine (Solis-Moreira, 2020). This success is a result of funding by several governments – such as that of the United States, where 'Operation Warp Speed' was launched along with public health agencies like the US Centers for Disease Control, international organizations such as the World Bank and the World Health Organization (WHO), and the private sector (Felter, 2021). All of these have played a significant role in expediting vaccine development.

To understand the complex processes involved in producing a vaccine, one must know more about the key actors: how much they invested, when and where, into promoting vaccine R&D. This information is critical for understanding the distribution of risks and potential rewards and the influence of R&D investments on who gets early access to its fruits – which can in turn help us think about how to prepare for future epidemics (GIIDS, 2021).

The scramble for vaccines during the covid crisis

Development of a COVID-19 vaccine became a priority for many scientists at numerous pharmaceutical and biotech companies around the world, eager to defeat the pandemic that was holding the world hostage. But this ambition was frustrated as it became apparent that poorer populations would not be included any time soon in the vaccination effort. Despite COVID-19 being perceived as a 'rich man's disease' or a high-class import that has been carried in by travellers (Bengali et al, 2020), the pandemic has grossly affected poorer nations in comparison to their rich counterparts, who in some cases had fewer infections but were the first to receive their doses. According to the Global Health Centre, the United States and Germany were the largest investors in vaccine R&D, along with other high-income countries (GIIDS, 2021). And while the United Kingdom was the first country to initiate a COVID-19 vaccination drive, the United States and Germany were also among the very first countries to gain access to large quantities of the vaccine (Al Jazeera, 2020). Buyers offering greater financial rewards were compensated with early access, even while other countries were facing more dire pandemic conditions.

The suggestion that pharmaceutical companies providing the vaccines were and are still partly driven by profits is not hyperbole when one considers which countries have been severely affected by the pandemic through the 'mismanagement' of vaccine distribution. An appeal made by the WHO in August 2021 called for a temporary halt in the administration of booster shots for COVID-19 vaccinations in rich countries due to rates of less than 2 per cent in vaccine distribution in low-income countries (LICs) in sharp contrast to high-income countries, where over 55 per cent have been fully vaccinated (*Nature*, 2021). In a variation of 'first come first serve', those who paid more or early (through financing R&D investment) received priority. Innovator firms' public declarations that they would help end the pandemic globally have not been reflected in their distribution policies. They have not provided early vaccine access to countries severely affected by the virus or ones where new disease variants were emerging. Instead, they have practised 'buyer favouritism' and have thereby increased their profits by selling at higher prices, prolonging the pandemic. In effect, they have followed the Friedmanian path.

Scaling up while preserving a demand–supply imbalance

As the pandemic has continued through several cycles of infection, Big Pharma has recognized the need for rapid mass production of vaccines. Scaling up vaccine production is an impressive feat for any pharmaceutical company, as lack of equipment, cost and time needed for licensing approval, shortages in essential components for the rapid scale up and poor strategic distribution of vaccines (Irwin, 2021) have previously prevented many firms from meeting their production targets. Pfizer and Moderna faced this problem with their commitment to manufacture and deliver 100 million doses at the beginning of the pandemic. In the months leading up to the delivery deadline, they had been steadily producing around 4.3 million doses a week instead of the 7.5 million they would have had to deliver to meet their target (Lupkin, 2021). This scaling up problem could have been solved by involving other firms in vaccine manufacturing on favourable terms. But the patent regime encourages innovators to keep their technologies and know-how to themselves in order to preserve their pricing power and reduce future competition.

Patents not merely secure the right to market one's product once it has received marketing approval. They also prevent others from selling the same product and often impede the development and marketing of similar, competing products through what is called strategic patenting (Gurgula, 2020). In this way, patents help capture market share, as exemplified by Pfizer/BioNTech and Moderna vaccines capturing 70 per cent of the total $36.907 billion in sales of COVID-19 vaccines and drugs in January–June 2021 (Philippidis, 2021).

Such patenting has not only hampered efforts to curb the spread of the virus but has also obstructed any form of capacity building. This limitation has barred the aiding and provision of innovative approaches to fighting the virus in LICs (Linn and Cooley, 2020) – so much so that the South African and Indian governments have requested that the intellectual property rights related to COVID-19 vaccines be suspended (Usher, 2020). Such a patent waiver would encourage LICs to invest in building capacity to manufacture their own affordable vaccines and alleviate the supply chain challenges discussed above. Many are opposed to this proposal, including Stephen J. Ubl, the President and CEO of the Pharmaceutical Research and Manufacturers of America, who fears that a patent waiver would cause financial loss for many firms (PhRMA, 2021).

The numerous issues and challenges that have been outlined thus far concerning pharmaceutical companies and their handling of the pandemic reveal an unfortunate pattern of vulnerable LICs being neglected when firms seek to maximize their profits from markups. Our experience with the COVID-19 pandemic closely parallels what would happen in a Friedmanian world of exclusively profit-maximizing firms. We need a better way of responding to epidemics, one that serves the needs of all.

A better approach to pandemic threats

How can we incentivize and reward pharmaceutical firms differently to make them perform better against pandemic threats? Their profits ought to track how well they serve human needs through fast containment and suppression of disease. For this purpose, such firms must solve a three-part task: quickly *develop* one or more pharmaceuticals that strongly protect from harm not merely treated patients but also the third parties whom these patients might infect; quickly *expand* manufacturing not only to meet market demand but all worldwide need for the new pharmaceutical(s), including the needs of the poorest; and then quickly *deliver* this manufactured supply in a strategic sequence calculated to crush the epidemic as quickly and thoroughly as possible.

What kind of reward system might provide optimal incentives to pharmaceutical firms? The most important objective here is to incentivize firms to fully include poor people in their strategy right from the start. For this to happen, an effective new pharmaceutical must be affordable to all, while delivering it even to the poorest must be profitable enough for firms to be eager to do so comprehensively and effectively. In our world of widespread poverty, these two requirements stand in tension. There is no sales price that is low enough to fulfil the former and high enough to fulfil the latter requirement. To resolve this tension, firms must receive a delivery premium in addition to the sales price. Such a premium, tied to health gain achieved, is an essential component of the Health Impact Fund approach, which offers firms performance rewards based on the real health gains achieved with any of their products, on condition that they sell this product without markup (Health Impact Fund, 2021).

Let us explore how this approach might be applied to the special case of vaccinating humankind against a pandemic disease. Here the core idea is to guarantee a reward payment for every indicated vaccination event anywhere. This guaranteed reward payment should be entirely independent of the economic position of the recipients or of their country and based solely on how vaccinations with a specific vaccine improve the health prospects of the person vaccinated and of other persons who might (directly or indirectly) become infected through this person. How large the aggregate health gain from vaccinating some given group of persons is depends on facts about the vaccine administered, the time of vaccination, the people vaccinated and their environment, including existing disease vectors.

It would evidently be impossible to assess the specific health gain achieved by each vaccination event individually. Fortunately, this is not necessary because the objective is not to ascertain the whole causal truth but to provide optimal incentives. For this purpose, reasonable approximations suffice. The reward should be sensitive to the extent to which a vaccination reduces the probability that its recipients will become infected and will infect others, and also sensitive to the extent to which it reduces the harm its recipients will suffer if they become infected despite having been vaccinated. These sensitivities result in a larger payment for vaccinations that are delivered sooner or provide better protection, including protection that works against more variants or remains effective for longer.

These sensitivities also entail higher rewards for delivering vaccinations to persons who are at higher risk of being infected or of infecting others – persons in high-incidence countries or regions, for instance, and persons in more interactive professional groups. However, such incentivizing differentiations in the reward per vaccination should be made only insofar as the vaccine provider is in charge of the relevant delivery decisions. If the vaccine supply is allocated by a national health service or by some international organization (such as the WHO or COVAX), then the reward should more simply be based on time of delivery and, mainly, on vaccine quality as manifested in its average impact given the general risk level prevailing in the relevant – national, regional or global – delivery population.

In the face of the COVID-19 epidemic, a timely guarantee that the vaccination of every vaccine-eligible person will be amply rewarded would have required a large reward pool, somewhere in the order of $50–100 billion, or 0.1–0.2 per cent of the combined gross national incomes of the affluent countries. This is substantially more than the few billions that COVAX has had at its disposal, enabling it to deliver around 1.4 billion doses as of 22 April 2022 (UNICEF, 2022), enough for about 700 million immunizations. But then the amount needed to back a universal guarantee is also vastly smaller than the economic damage this pandemic is causing worldwide and the national economic stimulus packages it has triggered, which are valued in the tens of trillions.

The proposed guarantee of universal vaccination would instantly remove any concern about whether vaccinating humanity's poorer half will be profitable. It would incline competing pharmaceutical innovators to seek to develop a highly effective vaccine and then to ramp up manufacture quickly to capture the largest-feasible share of the reward pool. When a firm's profit margin is essentially fixed, based on its manufacturing costs and the effectiveness of its vaccine, then this firm's profit depends on speed and quantity, on how many vaccinations are performed with its product. Each firm has an incentive, then, to effect delivery of its product as soon as possible. Firms would compete to use all available manufacturing capacity around the world and to expand such capacity towards accelerating deliveries.

These desirable incentives would be disturbed if some buyers were offering substantially higher per-dose payments in order to jump the queue. Such offers would cause departures from the optimal vaccination sequence – rich people with low infection risk would be vaccinated before even frontline health workers in poor countries. The prospect of such offers could also undermine the incentive for firms to deliver with maximum speed: slowness of manufacture and delivery prolongs the demand–supply imbalance that encourages and sustains a bidding war among rich buyers. Any such disturbance would make it harder to contain and suppress the pandemic globally, and rich countries ought therefore to subordinate their national interest to the best global strategy by agreeing to draw their vaccines solely from the single vaccine flow created by the global reward pool. In the present pandemic, they have utterly failed to do so. Thus far, about 8 per cent of vaccine doses have been distributed through COVAX and the remaining 92 per cent through a secretive bidding war among affluent buyers (UNICEF, 2022). No wonder, then, that the relevant pharmaceutical innovators are in no hurry to ramp up manufacture to immunize the world: potential profits from vaccinating the poorer half are small and doubtful, while large profits beckon from the continued demand–supply imbalance.

References

Al Jazeera (2020) 'Which countries have rolled out COVID vaccine?'. Available from: https://www.aljazeera.com/news/2020/12/24/vaccine-rollout-which-countries-have-started

Bengali, S., Linthicum, K. and Kim, V. (2020) 'How coronavirus – a "rich man's disease" – infected the poor', *Los Angeles Times*, 8 May. Available from: https://www.latimes.com/world-nation/story/2020-05-08/how-the-coronavirus-began-as-a-disease-of-the-rich

Felter, C. (2021) 'A guide to global COVID-19 vaccine efforts', Council on Foreign Relations, 1 April. Available from: https://www.cfr.org/backgrounder/guide-global-covid-19-vaccine-efforts

GIIDS (Graduate Institute of International and Development Studies) (2021) 'COVID-19 Vaccine R&D Investments'. Available from: https://www.knowledgeportalia.org/covid19-r-d-funding

Gurgula, O. (2020) 'Strategic patenting by pharmaceutical companies – should competition law intervene?', *IIC – International Review of Intellectual Property and Competition Law*, 51(9): 1062–85. Available from: https://doi.org/10.1007/s40319-020-00985-0

Health Impact Fund (2021) 'Delink the price of drugs from the cost of research'. Available from: https://healthimpactfund.org/en

Irwin, A. (2021) 'What it will take to vaccinate the world against COVID-19', *Nature*, 592(7853): 176–8. Available from: https://doi.org/10.1038/d41586-021-00727-3

Linn, L. and Cooley, L. (2020) 'Developing countries can respond to COVID-19 in ways that are swift, at scale, and successful', Brookings, 4 June. Available from: https://www.brookings.edu/blog/future-development/2020/06/04/developing-countries-can-respond-to-covid-19-in-ways-that-are-swift-at-scale-and-successful

Lupkin, S. (2021) 'Moderna and Pfizer need to nearly double COVID-19 vaccine deliveries to meet goals', NPR, 22 January. Available from: https://www.npr.org/sections/health-shots/2021/01/22/959732433/moderna-and-pfizer-need-to-nearly-double-covid-19-vaccine-deliveries-to-meet-goa

Mandeville, B. (1989 [1714]) *The Fable of the Bees*, Harmondsworth: Penguin Classics.

Nature (2021) 'The WHO is right to call a temporary halt to COVID vaccine boosters', 596(7872): 317. Available from: https://www.nature.com/articles/d41586-021-02219-w

Philippidis, A. (2021) 'Top 11 bestselling COVID-19 vaccines and drugs of H1 2021', GEN – Genetic Engineering and Biotechnology News. Available from: https://www.genengnews.com/a-lists/top-11-best-selling-covid-19-vaccines-and-drugs-of-h1-2021

PhRMA (2021) 'PhRMA statement on WTO TRIPS intellectual property waiver'. Available from: https://www.phrma.org/coronavirus/phrma-statement-on-wto-trips-intellectual-property-waiver

Smith, A. (2014 [1776]) *The Wealth of Nations*, Borehamwood: Shine Classics.

Solis-Moreira, J. (2020) 'COVID-19 vaccine: how was it developed so fast?', Medical News Today, 13 November. Available from: https://www.medicalnewstoday.com/articles/how-did-we-develop-a-covid-19-vaccine-so-quickly

UNICEF (2022) 'COVID-19 vaccine market dashboard'. Available from: https://www.unicef.org/supply/covid-19-vaccine-market-dashboard

Usher, A. (2020) 'South Africa and India push for COVID-19 patents ban', *The Lancet*, [online] 396(10265): 1790–1. Available from: https://www.thelancet.com/journals/lancet/article/PIIS0140-6736(20)32581-2/fulltext

PART III

Regional and Community Responses

NINE

Coping Mechanisms of Communities in Odisha: A Human Rights-Based Approach to the COVID-19 Pandemic

Nita Mishra, Sushree Sailani Suman and Anuradha Mohanty

This chapter examines the coping mechanisms used by communities in the state of Odisha in India during the COVID-19 pandemic period between 2020 and 2021. Using evidence of community participation facilitated by state policies and nongovernmental organizational (NGO) interventions, we show that a truly human rights-based approach to a pandemic such as COVID-19 is possible when communities seek to overcome challenges in sustainable ways.

The first section provides a brief theoretical understanding of rights-based approaches to development. In the second section, we use secondary literature sources to briefly describe initiatives and strategies adopted by the state government to combat COVID-19. This is followed, in the third section, by a focus on development activities initiated by the NGO People's Cultural Centre (PECUC) to ensure sustainable livelihoods, food security and the well-being of communities. This section draws from the authors' active fieldwork engagement in three districts of the state. The conclusion discusses the significance of shared duty-bearing obligations between the state government, NGOs and community-based groups in generating sustainable development for society as a whole.

A human rights-based approach

A human rights-based approach identifies a duty-bearer who is obligated to the rights-holder (members of vulnerable groups in society), who, in turn, has the right to demand fulfilment of a claim when denied or violated (Mishra, 2021). Scholars (Sen, 2004, 2009; Pogge, 2007; Sengupta, 2007) agree that the state, as the guarantor of rights, is the primary duty-bearer and has the primary obligation to fulfil and protect people's rights: 'So, Gods and saints were supposed to look after the poor, good kings were expected to protect the poor, and all virtuous were enjoined to help the poor' (Sengupta, 2007: 324).

Thus the task of benevolent duty-bearers is to look after, protect and help ordinary people and adopt specific measures to enable people to enjoy such rights (Sengupta, 2007: 329). However, despite moral imperatives, and the duties of the rulers, poverty persists, and rights are not fulfilled. Evidence from studies (Mishra and Lahiff, 2018) shows that to have rights secured from the state or other duty-bearers, people have to demand and claim constitutional rights (to life, food, livelihood and so on). As claims, rights impose a corresponding obligation on others, and such claims were validated by the person, the organization or the duty-bearer responsible for its smooth operation. 'Without the obligations there are no rights', argues O'Neill (2005: 431). Following from this is the argument that if there are obligations, there has to be a duty-bearer who is obliged to fulfil these obligations so that individuals can enjoy (constitutional) rights. Rights need to be claimed in situations where communities are not aware of constitutional rights (which is generally the case) nor of the means to realize those rights.

It is widely agreed that although the state is the primary duty-bearer, 'it cannot deliver the right on its own without taking into account the actions of all concerned social agents' (Sengupta, 2007: 329). Society consists of many 'interacting agents' such as corporates, NGOs, community-based organizations, faith-based organizations, women's groups and others. Sen (2004) makes it clear that claims to rights should be addressed generally to anyone who can help, and therefore, anyone who is in a position to help achieve human rights has a moral obligation to do so:

> The recognition of human rights is not an insistence that everyone everywhere rises to help prevent every violation of every human right no matter where it occurs. It is, rather, an acknowledgement that if one is in a plausible position to do something effective in preventing the violation of such a right, then one does have an obligation to consider doing just that. (Sen, 2004: 340–1)

Different duty-bearers, such as states, international institutions and other agents, will have different actions towards the same issue, such as responding to the COVID-19 pandemic for example. A feasible human rights-based approach to ensure food provisions, for instance, will therefore mean: there are obligations; these obligations are on duty-bearers who must be identified; the right-holders must be identified; there will be indicators to help identify these obligations or duties; and procedures will have to be laid down. Procedures include the setting up of administrative mechanisms and administrative structures through which food entitlement policies can be implemented at local levels so that citizens can access their right to food.

Furthermore, Sen emphasizes that if obligations are not clearly spelt out, it does not mean that there were none in the given context: 'Loosely specified obligations must not be confused with no obligations at all' (2004: 341). Thus, both

Sengupta and Sen broaden the scope of duty-bearers to include non-state actors and other members of civil society.

State government role in managing the COVID-19 pandemic

A quick survey of media reports and discussion documents (Sahoo and Kar, 2020: 373–87; WFP, 2021; WHO, 2020) shows that the Odisha state government ordered immediate closure of most public spaces on 13 March 2020 even before the first COVID-19 case was detected in the state on 15 March 2020 (a returnee from Italy). Odisha's track record of handling regular natural disasters, especially super-cyclones and floods, is credited for this quick thinking, wherein the Chief Minister along with the Natural Calamity Committee declared COVID-19 a 'state disaster' under its Disaster Management Act of 2005. This meant that officials at the district level across different government departments were empowered to act in their respective jurisdictions based on their information and experience (Das and Mishra, 2020; Sahoo and Kar, 2020). A strong governance response included the setting up of an Empowered Group of Ministers; 30 dedicated district-level COVID-19 hospitals, allowing health facilities to be independently assessed by World Health Organization (WHO) and UN teams adhering to infection prevention and control parameters; effective monitoring of government control rooms through reviews of surveillance; quarantine facilities; testing and treatment measures at the state, district and block level; engaging with the private sector to trace influenza-like illnesses and severe acute respiratory illnesses; deploying additional task forces including the state's administrative services officials, doctors, laboratory technicians and police personnel to contain the virus in high-risk districts; enhancing its testing capacity and patient care; leveraging technology (Sachetak and WhatsApp mobile applications) to monitor movement of cases and contacts through geographic information systems; dedicated call centres for public queries; and creating temporary medical camps that served as quarantine centres to accommodate 800,000 returning migrants to the state during the pandemic. These measures were complemented by affirmative state social welfare policies wherein pensions and other in-kind and cash benefits, including subsidized food entitlements to the poor, were delivered to the rights-holders well in advance so that the poor would not go hungry during the lockdown.

Two specific strategies adopted by the government of Odisha to combat the pandemic included, first, enlisting the support of NGOs and *panchayats* (village-level administration units), and the second was to engage with self-help groups (SHGs) of women to address the practical and strategic needs of vulnerable groups including returned migrants for access to food, shelter, healthcare and livelihoods. International organizations such as the WHO eventually published on its website how Odisha's government had managed to keep COVID-19 under control due to its effective governance and use of community-based strategies (Pradhan, 2020). The Odisha State Disaster Management Authority was one of the first government organizations in India to enlist the support of NGOs in not only raising awareness of the virus, assisting in quarantining affected people, but also in providing psycho-social counselling to the distressed and elderly population. Announcing its decision in a government circular dated 31 March 2020, the state additional chief secretary stated that 'NGOs are an important stakeholder in management of disasters and to provide tangible assistance to the district administration at the time of emergency' (Jena, 2020).

Using Section 51 of the National Disaster Management Act, 2005, 7 April 2020, the Chief Minister empowered *sarpanches* to ensure quarantine of returnees and their families, monitor the facilities and enlist the support of state volunteer workers, namely the local Anganwadi Workers (AWW) and Accredited Social Health Activists or ASHA workers (Sahoo, 2020). A *sarpanch* is the village head appointed by members of *panchayat*, which are village clusters and the lowest unit of the state administrative apparatus in India. Interestingly, the state government made the *sarpanches* take an oath to protect returnee migrant labourers on 22 April 2020, reflecting the empathetic approach taken by the government. In one district, the returnee migrants were given training to become community health workers in their quarantine centres (Sahoo and Kar, 2020). The ASHA workers have been key grassroots health workers along with the AWWs who assisted the local administration in contact tracing and managing the quarantine centres in villages.

The second significant government strategy was to involve the support of women's SHGs to assist with awareness generation, ensuring public health and hygiene and providing food security in rural and urban areas to poor and vulnerable groups during the lockdown period, which proved to be of immense benefit to the communities. According to studies (Patnaik et al, 2020; Patra, 2020; Sahoo and Kar, 2020), 1,339 SHGs have sewn around 7 million reusable masks for frontline workers and the poor, engaged in community kitchens to feed the poor and opened up vegetable shops in strategic locations to enable access by the vulnerable. In Odisha, women moved to the forefront of the battle against the pandemic. Seven million women of Mission Shakti have taken the lead in crucial initiatives responding to the pandemic, helping contain the spread of the virus by providing various community services (CDRI, 2020: 3).

Women's SHGs were created by the state government under the Mission Shakti programme in 2001, and later by NGOs with the sole purpose of empowering women through income-generating projects (Mishra, 2019; Mission Shakti, 2022). The key objective behind the formation of SHGs was to ensure that women can access institutional credit to enable self-employment through financial support in the form of seed money, loans and revolving funds. However, during the lockdown period, the small income generating projects came to a standstill, and families working in the informal sector were becoming food insecure. Noting the increased fear of starvation, PECUC officials decided to partner with the government, intervene and support the communities it worked with in three districts of Odisha.

More recently, the Department of Health and Family Welfare in Odisha (GOO, nd) has created a web portal on COVID-19 with updated information and animated videos, posters and pamphlets on numbers of people infected, resources for self-isolation at home for adults and children, self-registration for vaccines, support through telemedicine in all districts, pocketbooks on paediatric COVID for frontline workers, infection prevention and control and biomedical waste management in hospitals, among many other crucial interventions. According to the Health Services Director, B. Mohapatra: 'The condition will be under control if everyone continues following COVID-19 guidelines' (PTI, 2022). Daily rates of COVID-19 infection are very low: there were no reported deaths between 15 and 19 April 2020, for instance, from a population of 47.2 million, which reflects the success of state government initiatives as well as the active engagement of civil society itself in containing the spread of the disease (PTI, 2022).

People's Cultural Centre's women's self-help groups

Women's SHGs were key to PECUC strategy, as the NGO has been involved in the creation of more than 100 groups in the districts and had an active working relationship with women from different villages. The chief strategy used by PECUC was to empower communities to produce their own food and to share and exchange it for other basic needs among themselves. With the support of field workers from PECUC, women's SHGs took leadership roles in combatting hunger during the pandemic in the blocks of Balianta (Khordha district), Bhograin (Baleswar district) and in Patna (Keonjhar district) through a plethora of activities such as running community kitchens and producing and selling organic vegetables. Many SHGs engaged in *badi* making, making lentil flour, vegetable cultivation, mushroom cultivation, poultry, goatery, pottery, brass metalware, *pattachitra* (cloth-based scroll paintings with stories from religious mythologies in the state) and beetle vine production, commonly used with tobacco. Women opened grocery outlets selling homegrown vegetables, eggs and meat. Women's SHG members were involved in building awareness about handwashing practice and other safety measures related to COVID-19 mitigation as well. Although the negative impact of lockdown, closing of schools and loss of livelihood cannot be denied, the efforts made by the SHGs to counteract this impact reflects on the solidarity and agency of the women involved.

The second wave of the pandemic created turmoil and panic, leading to severe stress. In response to the panic created by the pandemic, the state government declared specific lockdown hours during which ordinary people could go out to shop for groceries and essentials. All commercial and public spaces including schools, colleges and other educational institutions were shut down from 5 May 2020 until 31 July 2020. People panicked more during the second phase because of their experience of the first lockdown, during which they had been forced to stay at home. In the second phase, the government ensured, in advance, that people living below the poverty line (BPL households) were provided with their basic needs' entitlements under a public distribution scheme. In short, pensions reached the poor, while food entitlements under the school midday meal schemes and cash transfers to pregnant women's accounts under various schemes were all honoured.

The PECUC Food Security Campaign between 15 December 2020 and 21 December 2020 was conducted in 52 villages with the direct participation of 11,237 people including government officials. The campaign involved walking in the villages with slogans and songs, organizing community meetings, mobile van campaigns with display messages, poster displays in strategic places, signature campaigns (petitions) and sharing and demonstrating traditional and nutritional vegetable recipes (PECUC, 2021: 5). Women's workload and stress, however, increased with restrictions on movement. Additionally, the economically weaker sections of the population – such as daily wage labourers – lost their work and sources of income, leading to household food scarcity and gender-based violence (Mohapatra, 2021).The second wave was reported as being more dangerous as more lives were lost. The print media, social media and television were showing a very grim picture, creating fear and suspicion among people with newspaper headlines claiming that a 'Third wave is coming'!

Women's groups have shown their solidarity in every sphere by actively involving themselves in combatting the pandemic. For example, the Mahila Adhikar Samukshya members of Bolgarh block cooked food for the extremely vulnerable and hungry groups of people who have been locally labelled as 'destitutes'. Women's SHG members took turns to help the state government in talking to migrant labourers who were returning to the villages from outside of Odisha. Support for returned migrants from NGOs such as PECUC was crucial for survival because many could not access government benefits owing to their 'neither here, not there' status (Behera et al, 2021). A total of 1,007,330 migrant workers returned to their respective villages during the pandemic. Of them, 181,702 workers were skilled workers and 554,754 were unskilled. Most returned migrant workers were from the textile, apparel and garment sector and the construction sector, according to the Labour and Employees Insurance Department. Mohapatra et al (2020) state that despite the affirmative steps such as arranging relief camps, transport buses, *shramik* (migrant labourers) special trains and quarantine measures for migrants undertaken by the government of Odisha, COVID-19 positive cases increased dramatically (Mohapatra et al, 2020). This led to questions about why migrants had not been brought back before lockdown when transmission of the virus was minimal to avoid mass infection. Others were concerned about the impact of the pandemic on migrants' mental health, as noted here: 'The Covid-19 pandemic has resulted in much psychological disorder among the seasonal migrants due to the harsh experience of travelling from the place of destination to the place of origin and related experiences' (Biswal, 2021).

The role of women's SHGs was important in combatting the pandemic. Almost all SHGs were engaged in sewing masks and selling them at low costs to fellow villagers. An interesting feature was the support of SHGs in the sale of perishable vegetables grown by poor farmers whereby '500 SHGs procured 171 tonnes of surplus produce from 15,000 farmers to supply to free kitchens and markets' (CDRI, 2020). According to Baisakh (2020a, b), one set of SHGs bought the farmers' produce and sold it to other SHGs, who took the produce for door-to-door sale in the villages. These perishable items were also delivered to the quarantined. State authorities acknowledged that the involvement of women in awareness generation, public health and ensuring food security not only promoted the livelihood of women SHGs but also helped in challenging gender stereotypes while showing new possibilities in enabling livelihood diversification (CDRI, 2020: 5).

Insights from interviews with small and marginal famers, migrants and daily wage earners undertaken by a World Food Programme report (2021: 42) found that people's access to food was limited by (a) the loss of livelihoods, which reduced their purchasing power and therefore their ability to get essential food commodities; (b) COVID-19-related lockdowns, which forced people to stay inside; and (c) restrictions limiting the availability of foods in shops, which led to increased food prices. Ensuring food security for vulnerable groups was a key area of intervention by SHGs. For example, '7312 SHGs have been engaged in free kitchen management, providing 19.1 million meals in urban and rural areas of the state' (CDRI, 2020: 4). Setting up businesses around the preparation and sale of dry fish as a nutritious supplement to food shortages was undertaken by Bhagabati SHG and Mahavir Women SHG group members of Andilo village of Balianta block, creating income for their families during the pandemic period. Discussions at the community level on nutritional self-dependency was an important activity that led to women's groups planting fruit trees and cultivating organic food crops. Many women's groups began cultivating organic vegetables and mushroom beds for their own consumption as well as sharing with neighbours and the needy. In Balianta block, a few SHGs started new activities such as beekeeping to produce their own honey. Women SHG groups of Mahukhanda (of Balianta block) were busy in beetle vine cultivation to help raise the income of their families. Creative outlets included making terracotta products as a cottage-based industry. In Balabhadrapur village (of Balianta block), Shakti Mahila SHG group decided to plant fruit trees to keep themselves active, challenge the stress of being locked down with the physical activity and produce their own fruits, as well as engaging in sustainable environmental development.

Participating in group meetings during the pandemic was an important way to come together in their own hamlet and share their lives with each other. It helped women relax and contributed to their mental health wellness. Women's groups from different districts of Odisha also participated in the 'Giliriphula' Forest Food Festival organized by tribal women's groups in the capital exhibition grounds during a less intense phase of the pandemic. PECUC also took the pandemic as an opportunity to engage women in advocacy campaigns, especially the Girl Advocacy and Alliance programme to raise awareness and prevent child trafficking and child marriage, and to promote secondary school education for girls and provide job-oriented vocational training for young women. Other campaigns were on preventing child labour, spreading awareness on COVID-19 Safety Protocol, handwash practising in their communities and volunteering their time to distribute food entitlements to the poor under the state public distribution system (PDS) and the pandemic relief distribution of PECUC. Under PECUC's involvement in the COVID-19 response programme, women participated and initiated awareness meetings, provided support in PDS distribution points in the districts of Balianta and Keonjhar, supported the government in pension distribution, identifying migrant labour and supporting them with dry rations, organic farming, organic kitchen gardens, mushroom cultivation, awareness generation, mask production, support in vaccination rollout, offering food to the destitute, collecting forest food and participation in the Forest Food Festival.

Women were also encouraged to participate in various online programmes and webinars organized by PECUC on gender issues, online safety and much more. They actively participated in the observation of National Anti-Child Labour Day, the webinar on 'Act Now: Stop Child Labour' on the occasion of World Day Against Child Labour on 12 June, a webinar on the occasion of World No Tobacco Day on 31 May and also participated in the state-level consultation on Nutritional Self-Dependence. In their area, they also observed World Earth Day on 22 April, World Water Day on 22 March, World Environment Day on 5 June and International Women's Day on 8 March while strictly following COVID-19 guidelines and protocol. More than 1,000 women actively engaged in various activities by PECUC. Women group members also participated in playing games like football and sack race competitions.

Women's groups in the blocks of Bolgarh, Balianta and Patna in the three districts also received training on income-generation activities, entrepreneurship and marketing, *pattachitra* making, brass metal object making, beekeeping, organic vegetable cultivation, nutrition training and poultry rearing. PECUC imparted training to women's SHG members in decision-making procedures of the Gram Sabha and Pallisabha, local village level administrative units. Women *panchayat* leaders received training in resource management in the Badakumari, Bankoidosh, Dihakhauruni, Sagargua, Baradandi, Patapursasan villages of Bolgarh block, and in the villages of Bainchua, Satyabhamapur, Posana, Gotalgram of Balianta block. PECUC managed to conduct in-person training of women leaders in the Balianta and Bolgarh block of Khordha district. An important area of work was to build capacities – including COVID-19 preventive measures – of the village-level government community workers, namely the AWW and ASHA in Bhograi block.

Youth engaging in COVID-19 relief activities

The youth 'as leaders and change makers' also participated in generating awareness on COVID-19 and the importance of getting vaccinated in the Young Warrior programme of UNICEF, spreading messages on social ills such as child labour and tobacco use through theatre and national- and state-level youth camps. Young people were busy organizing drinking water kiosks, the cleaning of village roads, canals and ponds. One of the key activities that drew a lot of media and government attention was the making of bird nests that attracted birds to the locality. These nests created by the youth group members of 'Ecosavers Youth Network' (EYN) of Jadichatar village of Swayampatna block of Keonjhar district received the attention of Honourable Chief Minister Mr Naveen Patnaik. This became a media sensation. Many leading news organizations, such as OTV, News 18, Kanak TV and Prameya News, visited Keonjhar to record the event.

Other youth groups, such as the Woodpecker EYN members in Baiganpal village of Ghatagaon block of Keonjhar district sprung up during the pandemic. These activities not only kept them engaged during the period but also provided them with a source of income. For instance, mushroom cultivation by EYN members of Badjamuposi village of Ghatagaon block earned them Rs 2,000–3,000 per month. EYN members prepared vermin compost and sold it in the local village to earn an income. Elsewhere, beekeeping has brought income to some. Training, tailored for youth, was organized by PECUC, for example in Patna block for frontline health workers, domestic data entry operators and masons were conducted. Training on online safety and career counselling were organized by PECUC. Other skills-based training was on organic farming, vermin in soil farming, mushroom cultivation, grocery and tailoring. Youth groups in PECUC-operational villages of blocks in Balianta, Bhubaneswar, Bhubaneswar slum and Patna actively participated in a plantation programme and planted more than 2,500 trees of local fruit-bearing species such as tamarind, mango, guava, jackfruit and Jamun.

At the government PDS, the youth supported the maintenance of COVID-19 protocols – such as maintaining physical distancing, handwashing and proper mask wearing during the distribution of dry rations of rice, wheat, sugar, oil, salt and kerosene to beneficiary PDS card holders, that is, people living under the poverty line. A village-wide beneficiary list was prepared in consultation with village committees along with other *panchayati raj* (village level administrative units) institution members. Items including soap, masks and sanitizers were distributed during the peak of the pandemic. Help from the youth in villages was also sought for the distribution of relief items by PECUC to economically poorer sections of society, especially daily wage earner families, single women headed families, older people families, child labour families, migrant labour families and physically disabled persons.

The youth, alongside PECUC, took the initiative to teach small children in their respective districts. Engaging children in the age group of five to 18 years of age of Balianta block, Bhubaneswar block, Bhubaneswar Municipal Corporation (BMC) slums, Patna block in spreading COVID-19 awareness messages and handwash practising was undertaken in creative ways such as drawing competitions, message writing and participation in various online activities of PECUC from homes. Various activities like involvement in the 44 days campaign to end child labour, awareness raising through writing eco-friendly messages on walls, including slogan writing such as 'Say no to child marriage' at Barsha of BMC slum, 'Send children to school not to work' (by Shaina of Balianta), and 'Tobacco companies kill their best customers'. PECUC also organized many online training programmes on gender issues, ecology and the environment, career counselling programmes for senior secondary students and organized sessions on online safety and counselling. To keep children active during lockdown phases, PECUC celebrated various days like World Earth Day, National Anti-Child Labour Day, World No Tobacco Day, World Environment Day, World Day Against Child Labour and Yoga day by strictly following COVID-19 protocols. More than 1,500 children were involved in creative activities and campaigns in all PECUC's operational areas.

In this chapter, we observe how NGOs such as PECUC have engaged with different sections of vulnerable communities despite the challenging circumstances imposed by the pandemic. The support of the state through affirmative policies such as taking immediate action, foresight, decentralizing its political and administrative authority and sharing responsibilities with other stakeholders, especially duty-bearers who find themselves 'in a plausible position to do something effective' (Sen, 2004: 340–1), was critical to combatting the pandemic. We have also shown that strategies to deal with COVID-19 can be sustainable only when communities take the responsibility to do so. Using detailed evidence from the development practice of PECUC in different districts, active community involvement in all regions and the critical role of the government in Odisha, we have shown that to be able to combat the COVID-19 pandemic, all members of a community need to act together, not only as rights-holders but also as duty-bearers.

References

Baisakh, P. (2020a) 'How self-help groups in rural Odisha helped both farmers and consumers during lockdown', *The Hindu.* Available from: www.thehindu.com/society/how-self-help-gro ups-in-rural-odisha-helped-both-farmers-and-consumers-dur ing-lockdown/article32294535.ece

Baisakh, P. (2020b) 'One Indian province proves the efficacy of decentralised governance in covid-management', *Open Democracy*. Available from: www.opendemocracy.net/en/openindia/one-ind ian-province-proves-efficacy-decentralised-governance-covid-management/

Behera, M, Mishra, S. and Behera, A.R. (2021) 'The COVID-19-led reverse migration on labour supply in rural economy: challenges, opportunities and road ahead in Odisha', *The Indian Economic Journal*, 69(3): 392–409.

Biswal, M. (2021) 'Crisis of seasonal migrants in Odisha during Covid-19 pandemic'. Available from: https://www.researchg ate.net/publication/350754685_Crisis_of_Seasonal_Migrants_ in_Odisha_during_Covid-19_Pandemic

CDRI (2020) 'Response to COVID-19 Odisha: Coalition for Disaster Resilient Infrastructure', National Disaster Management Authority. Available from: https://ndma.gov.in/sites/default/files/ PDF/covid/response-to-COVID-19-by-odisha.pdf

Das, A. and Mishra, S. (2020) 'Odisha's fight against COVID-19', University Practice Connect, Azim Premji University. Available from: https://practiceconnect.azimpremjiuniversity.edu.in/odis has-fight-against-covid-19/

GOO (nd) 'Detail status of Covid 19 (last updated on 20th April 2022), government of Odisha'. Available from: https://health. odisha.gov.in

GOO (nd) 'Covid training and resources, government of Odisha'. Available from: https://health.odisha.gov.in/tcbm.html

Jena, P. (2020) 'Collaborating with NGOs for mitigating negative effects of COVID-19', Letter 1152, Odisha State Disaster Management Authority, Bhubaneswar: OSDMA. Available from: https://health.odisha.gov.in/pdf/Collaborating-with-NGOs-mit igating-effect-COVID19-31-3-2020.pdf

Mishra, N. (2019) 'Understanding empowerment through perceptions of self-help group women in Odisha', *Research & Perspectives on Development Practice*, 23. Available from: https:// mural.maynoothuniversity.ie/10991

Mishra, N. (2021) 'Operationalizing rights-based approaches to development: chinks in the armour observed through a study of anganwadi workers in Odisha, India', in S. Egan and A. Chadwick (eds), *Poverty and Human Rights: Multidisciplinary Perspectives*, London: Edward Elgar, 171–87.

Mishra, N. and Lahiff, E. (2018) 'We are the locals: the operationalisation of rights-based approaches to development by non-governmental organisations in Koraput District, Odisha', *European Journal of Development Research*, 30(5): 809–22.

Mohapatra, D. (2021) '29% rise in rape cases in first half of 2021 in Odisha', *Times of India*, 7 September. Available from: https://timesofindia.indiatimes.com/city/bhubaneswar/29-rise-in-rape-cases-in-1st-half-of-2021/articleshow/85985396.cms

Mohapatra, R.K., Das, P.K. and Kandi, V. (2020) 'Challenges in controlling COVID-19 in migrants in Odisha, India', *Diabetes Metab Syndr*, 14(6) (November–December): 1593–9.

O'Neill, O. (2005) *Justice, Trust and Accountability*, Cambridge: Cambridge University Press.

Patnaik, A., Sharma, A. and Mohanty, A. (2020) 'Odisha has emerged as an underrated leader in Covid-19 management', The Wire, 5 May. Available from: https://thewire.in/government/odisha-covid-19-management

Patra, S. (2020) 'How Odisha's "Mission Shakti" women are at the forefront of the battle against COVID-19', Times Now, 27 April. Available from: https://www.timesnownews.com/columns/article/how-odisha-s-mission-shakti-women-are-at-the-forefront-of-the-battle-against-covid/583466

PECUC (2021) 'Annual report 2020–2021', Bhubaneswar: People's Cultural Centre.

Pogge, T. (2007) 'Introduction', in T. Pogge (ed), *Freedom from Poverty as a Human Right: Who Owes What to the Very Poor?*, Oxford: Oxford University Press, 11–54.

Pradhan, A. (2020) 'Odisha's response to Covid earns praise from WHO', *Times of India*, 1 October. Available from: https://timesofindia.indiatimes.com/city/bhubaneswar/odishas-response-to-covid-earns-praise-from-who/articleshow/78419452.cms

PTI (2022) 'COVID situation stable in Odisha, mask mandate yet to be lifted', *New Indian Express*, Press Trust of India, 19 April. Available from: https://www.newindianexpress.com/states/odisha/2022/apr/19/covid-situation-stable-in-odisha-mask-mandate-yet-to-be-lifted-2443888.html

Sahoo, N. and Kar, M.R. (2020) 'Evaluating Odisha's COVID-19 response: from quiet confidence to a slippery road', *Journal of Social and Economic Development* 23(2): 373–87. Available from: https://www.ncbi.nlm.nih.gov/pmc/articles/PMC7687211

Sahoo N. (2020) 'Panchayats and pandemic: ORF analysis'. Observer Research Foundation, 25 April. Available from: https://www.orfonline.org/expert-speak/panchayats-pandemic-65185

Sen, A. (2004) 'Elements of a theory of human rights', *Philosophy and Public Affairs*, 32(94): 315–56.

Sen, A. (2009) *The Idea of Justice*, Cambridge: Belknap Press of Harvard University Press.

Sengupta, A. (2007) 'Poverty eradication and human rights', in T. Pogge (ed), *Freedom from Poverty as a Human Right: Who Owes What to the Very Poor?*, Oxford: Oxford University Press, 323–44.

Sharma, R. (2022) 'Odisha Mission Shakti 2022: Application Form PDF, Eligibility & Benefits' in PM Modi Yojana. Available from: https://pmmodiyojana.in/odisha-mission-shakti/

WFP (2021) 'Assessment of food security among vulnerable groups in Odisha during COVID-19', World Food Programme, February. Bhubaneshwar: World Food Programme.

WHO (2020) 'From governance to community resilience: Odisha's response to COVID-19', World Food Programme, 17 September. Available from: https://www.who.int/india/news/feature-stories/detail/from-governance-to-community-resilience-odisha-s-response-to-covid-19

TEN

To Lockdown or Not to Lockdown: A Pragmatic Policy Response to COVID-19 in Zambia

Chrispin Matenga and Munguzwe Hichambwa

It is now more than two years since COVID-19 was declared a pandemic by the World Health Organization (WHO). The pandemic spread geographically with great speed and a high rate of mortality, initially in the high- and middle-income countries, but more recently in the developing world (Carmody and McCann, 2020: 1–6; Haider et al, 2020). In response to the pandemic, many countries around the world instituted policy measures and 'lockdowns' of various sorts to contain it. Globally, the policy responses to contain the virus have been similar but were applied by individual countries with different levels of intensity in line with the evolution of the pandemic in the countries concerned. There are arguments that the universalized lockdown measures were likely to have little or no benefits for developing countries compared to the wealthier countries of the Global North due to their differing social and economic contexts (Cannon, 2020). In this chapter, we examine Zambia's policy response and lockdown measures in the context of the uncertainties over the consequences of adopting hard lockdown measures. The state's response to COVID-19 in Zambia, we argue, has been highly pragmatic and more measured against its economic circumstances rather than 'going with the wind'. The research starts from the premise that most of Zambia's people eke out a livelihood from the informal economy. This chapter, therefore, aims to analyse the nature of COVID-19 lockdown measures adopted by the Zambian state and the rationale informing the adoption of this type of response, looking at how policies and measures have served to protect the livelihoods of the majority of the people in a highly informal economy.

The emergence of COVID-19

The emergence of COVID-19 in China in late 2019 and its global spread in early 2020 caught the world by surprise. The speed with which the pandemic spread geographically, and its high rate of mortality, prompted many countries around the world to institute 'lockdowns' of various sorts to contain it (Carmody and McCann, 2020; Haider et al, 2020). As MacGregor, Ripoll and Leach (2020: 115) argue, conventional epidemic response frameworks are based on what they term an 'outbreak narrative' that 'focuses on particular disease dynamics – "sudden emergence, speedy, far-reaching, [and often] global spread" – and on particular types of response – "universalised, generic emergency-oriented control, at source, aimed at eradication"'. The concern 'is the reality of limited knowledge about many aspects of outbreaks, coupled with predictions of potentially devastating consequences – both rapidly unfolding and fatal' (MacGregor, Ripoll and Leach, 2020: 113). For instance, there was uncertainty on the main channels of transmission of COVID-19, the number of people infected, the number of potential fatalities and the economic and social consequences that various policy options would imply (Boin and Lodge, 2021).

The first case of COVID-19 was identified in Zambia on 18 March 2020. The first few months following this confirmed case of COVID-19 were characterized by a slow spread of the disease, and cases remained relatively low. For instance, as of 15 April 2020, the country had reported 48 confirmed cases and two deaths (ZNPHI, 2020a). Confirmed cases rose to 668 and deaths to seven by 15 May 2020 (ZNPHI, 2020b). When some COVID-19 measures began to be lifted in May 2020, however, Zambia experienced exponential growth in cases, particularly during the month of July. Confirmed COVID-19 cases rose from 1,632 on 6 July to 4,481 on 26 July (OCHA, 2020a). This increase in numbers forced Parliament to adjourn prematurely, particularly after two legislators succumbed to the disease. By 29 October 2020, the country had reported 16,325 cases and 348 deaths (OCHA, 2020b), which signalled the start of what was characterized as a 'second wave'. As of 23 February 2021, the second wave had peaked, with the country recording 75,582 cases and 1,040 deaths (ZNPHI, 2021a). Cases began to abate between March and April 2021 but then rose again in May, with a warning that a third wave was imminent. The month of June 2021 could be described as the COVID-19 'apocalypse' for Zambia, as the rise in cases and deaths was unprecedented (Matenga and Hichambwa, 2021). On 20 June 2021, the country recorded 2,060 new cases and 49 deaths in the preceding 24 hours, bringing the cumulative confirmed cases to 129,033 and cumulative deaths to 1,644 (ZNPHI, 2021b).

COVID-19 policy choices and lockdown measures

In the wake of the pandemic, the term 'lockdown' has become a catchphrase. Global health institutions such as the WHO have been instrumental in guiding countries on various measures that should be put in place to prevent and/ or reverse the transmission of the virus. Despite this effort by the world health body, there has not yet been a precise definition of what characterizes 'lockdown'. Thus, as Haider et al (2020: 2) note, several adjectives for the term – such as 'total lockdown', 'partial lockdown', 'hard lockdown' and 'soft lockdown' – have been used but without clear definitions. In this chapter, we adopt the definition elaborated by Haider et al (2020: 2), which views lockdowns as a 'set of measures aimed at reducing transmission of COVID-19 that are mandatory, applied indiscriminately to a general population and involve some restrictions on the established pattern of social and economic life'. These authors further isolate three elements within this definition to give a precise meaning to the term 'lockdown'. These are: (i) geographic containment, (ii) home confinement and (iii) prohibition of gatherings and closure of establishments and premises (Haider et al, 2020).

The emergence of COVID-19 triggered a crisis for which national leaders had to make policy choices about how to forestall the transmission of the virus. However, making policy choices in the midst of uncertainty bedevils many political leaders globally (Boin and Lodge, 2021). Of great concern to political leaders during the COVID-19 crisis has been the approach to follow to prevent or minimize the spread of COVID-19 and the socioeconomic consequences these policy choices would entail. Political leaders are confronted by two ideal-typical approaches to crisis decision-making: the principled and the pragmatic approach. Generally, the principled approach adopts a guiding core principle or value in decision-making. For instance, a decision-maker can aim to 'minimize harm on the health of the people' or 'minimize harm on economic and social life'. On the other hand, the pragmatic approach envisages 'an experimental, trial-and-error strategy that relies on a mixture of reasoning and feedback: try something that appears likely to work, study the consequences, and adjust where necessary' (Boin and Lodge, 2021: 1132). Globally, the policy guidelines on the containment of COVID-19, while similar, have varied in application by individual countries depending on the approach taken. The measures have included closure of borders, stay-at-home orders, curfews, travel bans and total or partial lockdowns. Others include frequent handwashing or use of alcohol-based hand sanitizers, physical distancing, use of masks in public places and restrictions on the number of people attending public gatherings (WHO, 2020).

While the global concern in the early months following the emergence of COVID-19 was with health impacts, some studies suggest that the lockdown measures put in place by governments were likely to cause more harm than the actual virus itself (Carreras et al, 2020; GHI, 2020). Additionally, data suggest that the socioeconomic shocks arising from lockdowns have been more severe in Sub-Saharan Africa than other regions in the world, generating dire livelihood consequences for most citizens who depend on the informal economy for survival (Carmody and McCann, 2020; McCann and Matenga, 2020). Some observers note that several factors combine to explain the severity of harm resulting from the lockdowns. These include the breadth, depth and length of the measures put in place by governments; the state of the economy preceding the emergence of COVID-19; and levels of fear about COVID-19 in respective countries (Haider et al, 2020: 7). The breadth of lockdown measures relates to the volume or how widespread the measures are. Depth relates to the intensity of application of these measures, while length relates to the duration of the measures remaining in effect during the pandemic.

COVID-19 lockdown measures in Zambia

Following the global 'outbreak narrative' (MacGregor et al, 2020), and in anticipation of the emergence of COVID-19 in the country, the Zambian government gazetted orders to manage the spread of the pandemic as well as other policy responses to mitigate pandemic associated negative socioeconomic impacts. On 13 March 2020, the government issued Public Health Statutory Instruments '21 and 22 of 2020' to aid the enforcement of lockdown measures that the government anticipated to announce and at the same time approved a COVID-19 contingency and response plan, and a budget (AGRA, 2020).

Uncertainty surrounding COVID-19 and the initially low numbers of confirmed cases in the period following the outbreak and low fatalities at the time prompted a national debate as to whether it was public health or the economy and livelihoods that the government should care more about, as it weighed different policy options in curbing the spread of the virus. A cross-section of people, including some opposition political parties, began calling for a total lockdown to safeguard public health when cases began escalating. The government authorities, however, refused to impose a total lockdown, claiming that it would have a worse outcome than COVID-19 itself (Mvula, 2020), and embraced a more pragmatic approach in dealing with the pandemic. The government instead opted for 'a phased strategy that will take into consideration interventions for the low and high income groups, low and high density areas, rural and urban areas' (GRZ, 2020). The government argued that a total lockdown would result in severe livelihood consequences given most of the population's dependence on the informal economy for daily survival (GRZ, 2020), with the informal sector in Zambia accounting for 69 per cent of the labour force (ZSA and MLSS, 2020).

Before the onset of the COVID-19 pandemic, the Zambian economy was projected to experience negative growth in 2020, dropping by at least 2.6 per cent. The country's poor economic performance was triggered by a severe drought in 2018 and, together with declining mining activity, resulted in the gross domestic product dropping from 4 per cent growth in 2018 to 1.5 per cent in 2019 (AGRA, 2020). The impact of this drought on agricultural and hydroelectricity production, and a fall in copper prices due to reduced global demand as a result of COVID-19, has led Zambia's economy to enter a downward spiral. Together with rising debt due to government over-borrowing, this has caused a severe economic crisis. The national currency, the Zambian Kwacha, had been depreciating in the years prior to the pandemic, and by one estimate had depreciated by about 50 per cent on a yearly basis by October 2020 (FAO, 2020). It was thus clear that the impacts of COVID-19 and an economy under pressure were self-reinforcing, and a total lockdown would have aggravated these negative impacts.

On 17 March 2020, prior to the announcement of the first COVID-19 case in the country, the government ordered the closure of all learning institutions, including schools, colleges and universities (GRZ, 2020). On 25 March 2020, after the first case of COVID-19 was detected, the government announced the first major package of lockdown measures. The measures included those focused largely on controlling international travel to prevent further 'importation' of COVID-19 cases into the country, while others were more inward looking. Thus, Zambian missions abroad and the department of immigration were ordered to review the issuance of visas for people wanting to travel to Zambia and at all ports of entry into the country for all travellers from countries affected by COVID-19. All international flights were to land at the main international airport in the capital city Lusaka and all travellers were to be screened for COVID-19 at points of entry. Those exhibiting symptoms were to be quarantined. Non-essential foreign travel to countries that had confirmed COVID-19 cases were suspended (GRZ, 2020; Haider et al, 2020).

Other measures focused on internal business operations that attracted gatherings and were likely to be COVID-19 transmission hotspots. The internally focused lockdown measures included the closure of gyms, bars, nightclubs, cinemas and casinos, while restaurants were to operate on a takeaway basis only. However, most businesses, particularly those dealing with essential goods and services including all shops, food markets and supermarkets, were allowed to continue operating throughout the pandemic. Religious gatherings were banned, while public gatherings such as conferences, weddings, funerals and festivals were restricted to no more than 50 participants and required authorization by local authorities through a permit (GRZ, 2020). Furthermore, governmental authorities issued stay-at-home appeals and ordered non-essential workers to work from home and others to work on a rational basis. These measures were periodically reviewed. The periodic reviews of the lockdown measures allowed for feedback from public health officials, enabling the government to adjust where necessary, a hallmark of the country's pragmatic approach to the COVID-19 crisis. Thus, over time during the pandemic, some restrictions have been relaxed and restored a number of times depending on the way the pandemic has progressed. Some of the restrictions, such as the closure of international airports, were relaxed completely early on in the pandemic in June 2020. Over and above lockdown measures, the government also issued public health guidelines that included the wearing of masks, frequently washing hands or use of alcohol-based hand sanitizers, maintaining physical/social distance and avoiding handshakes.

An illuminating feature of Zambia's lockdown is the absence of any wide-ranging geographic containment in people's movements or curfew to contain the spread of COVID-19 – as has been the case in South Africa, Zimbabwe, Uganda, Rwanda and Botswana (Haider et al, 2020). The 'stay at home' appeals were a voluntary measure and not mandatory, and people therefore had the freedom to move anywhere in the country as they wished throughout the pandemic. Thus, most businesses in the informal sector including trade and services and agricultural production continued to operate throughout the pandemic, which allowed most people to continue earning income as before the pandemic. Nonetheless, the country implemented two very brief movement restrictions involving two districts during the 'first COVID-19 wave'. The first 'mini-lockdown' was in Kafue district bordering the capital city Lusaka, which took place for just one day on 15 April 2020 to allow health authorities to carry out some targeted testing after the district recorded three cases and was deemed a COVID-19 epicentre during the early days of the pandemic (Siame, 2020). A second example was the brief border closure with Tanzania and partial lockdown of the border area in Nakonde from 11 May to 15 May 2020 following an escalation of cases among truck drivers and the community at the border area and its designation as the new epicentre at the time (AGRA, 2020; Haider et al, 2020). Other than these two targeted lockdowns, there has not been any ban on interdistrict or interprovincial movement of people and public transportation. Nevertheless, the public exercised self-restraint in making movements from fear of getting infected by COVID, as little was known at the time about the transmission channels.

However, once COVID-19 cases and deaths abated, following a presidential and general election in August 2021, the new United Party for National Development (UPND) government that defeated the Patriotic Front (PF) government remained aloof in enforcing the lockdown measures and eventually announced a complete rollback of these measures starting 1 October 2021. This was except for the public health guidelines on the wearing of masks, frequently washing hands, sanitizing and physical distancing. On 28 November 2021, following the discovery of a new COVID-19 variant – Omicron – in Southern Africa in the same month, the UPND government restored the measures rolled back within a space of one month and went further going into 2022 to mandate all those requiring access to government buildings to show evidence of COVID-19 vaccination and all civil servants in the country to be vaccinated for COVID-19 for them to be admitted to work (GRZ, 2021).

Like many other countries around the world, Zambia took decisions on the types of COVID-19 lockdown measures to embrace. Confronted by the many uncertainties surrounding the trajectory of the pandemic and its consequences, the Zambian political leadership had to weigh its choices amid these uncertainties. Thus, Zambia's pragmatic COVID-19 policy choices and lockdown measures were not only a reflection of the country's constrained fiscal space but also of political considerations by the PF regime given that the country was heading towards a presidential and general election on 12 August 2021. Imposing a hard lockdown would have alienated the party from its strategic support base that largely ekes out a livelihood from the informal sector and, therefore, would risk PF losing the impending election. Political considerations aside, the pragmatic approach embraced by the government assisted in protecting the livelihoods of those who rely on the informal sector for their daily earnings. At the same time, apart from short periods of escalating COVID-19 cases in the country, just like in many other countries in the region, the much feared health crisis failed to materialize, at least in the medium term compared to many Western countries that took a principled approach accompanied by hard lockdown measures but are still struggling with escalating cases despite the huge uptake of COVID-19 vaccines. The pragmatic approach taken by the Zambian state not only allowed for less stringent lockdown measures but also early easing up of the measures informed by evidence from public health officials. As the COVID-19 pandemic is ever evolving, countries are confronted with 'twists and turns' in this crisis and, therefore, lockdown measures are best informed within a framework of active learning that renders fewer negative socioeconomic consequences than taking a harder, more rigid approach likely to cause more socioeconomic harm.

References

AGRA (2020) 'COVID-19 pandemic and its impact on agriculture and food security – policy response for Zambia'. Available from: https://agra.org/wp-content/uploads/2020/06/Zambia-COVID-19-Policy-Response-Package_June2020.pdf

Arjen Boin, A. and Lodge, M. (2021) 'Responding to the COVID-19 crisis: a principled or pragmatist approach?', *Journal of European Public Policy*, 28(8): 1131–52.

Cannon, B. (2020) 'COVID-19 in Latin America: uneven responses, uneven impacts, shared challenges', in P. Carmody, G. McCann, C. Colleran and C. O'Halloran (eds), *Rapid Response: COVID-19 in the Global South, Impacts and Responses*, Bristol: Bristol University Press.

Carmody, P. and McCann, G. (2020) 'Introduction', in P. Carmody, G. McCann, C. Colleran and C. O'Halloran (eds), *Rapid Response: COVID-19 in the Global South, Impacts and Responses*, Bristol: Bristol University Press.

Carreras, M., Saha, A. and Thompson, J. (2020) 'Rapid assessment of the impact of COVID-19 on the food systems and rural livelihoods in Sub-Saharan Africa', *APRA COVID-19 Synthesis Report 2*, Brighton: Future Agricultures Consortium.

FAO (2020) 'GIEWS country brief Zambia', Food and Agricultural Organization of the United Nations. Available from: http://www.fao.org/giews/en

GHI (Global Hunger Index) (2020) *Global Hunger Index (GHI)*, Bonn and Dublin: Welt Hunger Hilfe and Concern Worldwide.

GRZ (Government Republic of Zambia) (2020) 'Statement by His Excellency, Dr. Edgar Chagwa Lungu, president of the Republic of Zambia on the COVID-19 pandemic', 25 March. Available from: https://www.mof.gov.zm/download/speeches

GRZ (2021) 'Statement on COVID-19 in Zambia Lusaka', 28 November. Available from: http://www.moh.gov.zm

Haider, N., Osman, A.Y., Gadzekpo, A., Akipede, G.O., Asogun, D., Ansumana, R. et al (2020) 'Lockdown measures in response to COVID-19 in nine sub-Saharan African countries', *BMJ Global Health* 5 (2020): e003319. Doi:10.1136/bmjgh-2020–003319.

MacGregor, H., Ripoll, S. and Leach, M. (2020) 'Disease outbreaks: navigating uncertainties in preparedness and response', in I. Scoones and A. Stirling (eds), *The Politics of Uncertainty: Challenges of Transformation*, London: Routledge.

Matenga, C. and Hichaambwa, M. (2021) 'A multi-phase assessment of the effects of COVID-19 on food systems and rural livelihoods in Zambia', *APRA COVID-19 Country Report*, Brighton: Future Agricultures Consortium. Available from: https://doi.org/10.19088/APRA.2021.039

McCann, G. and Matenga, C. (2020) 'COVID-19 and global inequality', in P. Carmody, G. McCann, C. Colleran and C. O'Halloran (eds), *Rapid Response: COVID-19 in the Global South, Impacts and Responses*, Bristol: Bristol University Press.

Mvula, S. (2020) 'Lockdown deadlier', *Zambia Daily Mail Limited*, 8 August. Available from: http://www.daily-mail.co.zm/lockdown-deadlier

OCHA (United Nations Office for the Coordination of Humanitarian Affairs) (2020a) 'Zambia situation report', 29 July, New York: OCHA. Available from: https://data.humdata.org/visualization/covid19-humanitarian-operations

OCHA (United Nations Office for the Coordination of Humanitarian Affairs) (2020b) 'Zambia situation report', 29 October, New York: OCHA. Available from: https://data.humdata.org/visualization/covid19-humanitarian-operations

Siame, N. (2020) 'Kafue in lockdown', *Zambia Daily Mail Limited*, 15 April.

WHO (World Health Organization) (2020) 'Novel coronavirus (2019-nCoV) advice for the public', World Health Organization. Available from: https://www.google.com/search?client=firefox-b-d&q=WHO+%28World+Health+Organization%29+%282020%29+%E2%80%98Novel+Coronavirus+%282019-nCoV%29+Advice+for+the+Public%E2%80%99

ZNPHI (Zambia National Public Health Institute) (2020a) 'Daily status update, 15 April 2020', ZNPHI. Available from: https://www.africanews.com/2020/04/16/coronavirus-zambia-covid-19-status-update-15-april-2020 (webpage no longer available, information correct at time of access)

ZNPHI (2020b) 'Daily status update, 15 May 2020', ZNPHI. Available from: https://www.africanews.com/2020/05/15/ coronavirus-zambia-status-update-15th-may-2020 (webpage no longer available, information correct at time of access)

ZNPHI (2021a) 'Daily status update, 23 February, 2021', ZNPHI. Available from: http://znphi.co.zm/news/wp-content/uploads/ 2021/02/Zambia_COVID-Situational-Report-No-150_23Feb ruary2021_Final.pdf (webpage no longer available, information correct at time of access)

ZNPHI (2021b) 'Daily status update, 20 June 2021'. ZNPHI. Available from: https://twitter.com/ZMPublicHealth/status/ 1406557708292067330?s=20+Institute%29+%282021b%29+ %E2%80%98Daily+Status+Update%2C+20+June%2C+ 2021%E2%80%99 (webpage no longer available, information correct at time of access)

ZSA (Zambia Statistics Agency) and MLSS (Ministry of Labour and Social Security) (2020) 'Republic of Zambia 2019 labour force survey report'. Available from: https://www.zamstats.gov. zm/phocadownload/Labour/2019%20Labour%20Force%20Rep ort.pdf

ELEVEN

Latin America: Politics in Times of COVID-19

Salvador Martí i Puig and Manuel Alcántara Sáez

The aim of this chapter is to outline the response of institutions and social and political actors of the countries of Latin America to the COVID-19 pandemic. The impact of the pandemic on democracy is also analysed in the knowledge that decisions taken during the pandemic may have been similar to those that triggered the stock market crash of 1929, the 1973 oil crisis and the 1982 debt crisis. We have based this research on the assumption that the health crisis has represented a crucial turning point insofar as it has generated a situation of uncertainty in which the response of the most relevant political, social and economic actors in each country has been key in determining subsequent political and institutional development. The literature (Mahoney, 2000; Alcántara, 2020a) claims that this situation has entailed new social realignments and political coalitions, economic decision-making that is different from what was previously implemented as well as different wars of ideas – all of which signal the beginning of a new era.

In this respect, the health crisis that began in Wuhan, China, as a result of the outbreak of a new type of virus (COVID-19) at the end of 2019 has led to a situation of crisis in most countries around the world. In response to the pandemic, governments in almost every country worldwide have established containment measures and suspended social and economic activities, as well as closing borders. But over and above the health emergency, the crisis has revealed multiple structural limitations of a different nature, as well as the demagoguery of a considerable number of political authorities.

This scenario has also played out in Latin America, where, although the pandemic arrived a month later (see Table 11.1 for the key dates of the pandemic in the region), its after-effects were more devastating than in any other region of the world. As of 20 April 2022, in absolute terms, Brazil was third in the world (after the United States and India) in terms of number of infections and the second in deaths (30,279,270 and 662,266, respectively), with Mexico having the fifth highest number of deaths (323,973) and Peru the sixth highest (212,676) worldwide.[1]

The health crisis in Latin America came at a difficult moment for the economy and society. In 2019, the economy was deteriorating, and growth forecasts were only modest. After starting the 21st century with a long decade of growth (from 2000 to 2012), referred to as the commodities boom, this cycle ran out of steam, and with the fall in tax revenues, many anti-poverty policies were ended when they were most needed.

The response to the crisis: the reaction of governments, political and social actors

There has been considerable variability in the response to the COVID-19 health crisis among governments, political and social actors in each of the countries. Reactions have varied according to timelines, strategic decision-making, constructed narratives, the capacity and willingness to promote public policies and the objectives of each government.

With a view to analysing governmental responses, in this section we have classified the actors that first 'communicated' the outbreak of the health crisis and how it was being managed, the type of discourse they constructed, whether they

Table 11.1: COVID-19 key dates and number of deaths in Latin America

Country	Date of first case in 2020	Date of first death in 2020	Date of first 'Suspension of Guarantees' in 2020	Number of deaths per million inhabitants *
Argentina	3 March	7 March	19 March	2.285
Bolivia	10 March	28 March	21 March	1.901
Brazil	26 February	18 March	Not implemented	3.131
Chile	3 March	20 March	18 March	2,998
Colombia	6 March	16 March	17 March	2.774
Costa Rica	6 March	18 March	16 March	1.649
Cuba	11 March	18 March	Not implemented	751
Ecuador	29 February	13 March	16 March	2.040
El Salvador	18 March	31 March	14 March	638
Guatemala	13 March	15 March	6 March	1.044
Honduras	11 March	27 March	16 March	1.116
Mexico	27 February	18 March	Not implemented	2.534
Nicaragua	18 March	26 March	Not implemented	35
Panama	9 March	10 March	13 March	1.924
Paraguay	7 March	20 March	16 March	2.658
Peru	6 March	19 March	15 March	6.533
Dominican Republic	22 February	16 March	20 March	407
Uruguay	13 March	28 March	Not implemented	2.072
Venezuela	13 March	26 March	17 March	199

Source: Martí and Alcántara (2020: 13) and worldmeter.info/coronavirus

* Data from 7 April 2022. Data from some countries (notably Nicaragua and Venezuela) are inconsistent with reality.

Source: https://www.statista.com/statistics/1104709/coronavirus-deaths-worldwide-per-million-inhabitants maintained the same discourse throughout the crisis and the type of media used to deliver their messages. This is followed by a discussion of the institutions and actors' that assumed leadership in the crisis, noting the relevance of the head of state, the prime minister (or similar position if there is one) and the legislative or judicial authority. Thirdly, the role of political and social actors in the crisis is highlighted, be they the opposition, the media, organized civil society or community initiatives. Finally, based on this discussion, some tentative conclusions will be offered in the final section, reflecting on the impact of the crisis on the state of the region's democracies.

Who communicated with the public and how?

As mentioned, the first thing to establish are the actors who communicated the outbreak of the virus and measures to manage the health crisis, the type of discourse they adopted and the channels used to convey the information. In this context, it should be noted that all governments have operated in a situation of confusion, improvisation and a rapid depletion of available resources.

As a result, in the first few weeks of the pandemic a sense of fear was generated, which governments had to counteract by means of communication policies aimed at reassuring citizens. Table 11.2 shows how governments fared in the area of communications.

Table 11.2 shows how, in all cases, the president appealed to and asserted the 'nation' with a strong emotional content. All the heads of states embraced their national flag in an attempt to close ranks in the face of an unknown and invisible enemy coming from outside. Only in this way can the patriotic rhetoric deployed with reference to 'unity' be understood. However, this does not mean that all presidents have been equally active in the media. It is true that most have taken centre stage, and the fact that some of them were infected with the virus has added to the emotion of their media appearances.

Table 11.2: Government communications in response to the COVID-19 crisis

Country	The President was responsible for communicating with the public	Presence of another major actor	War/religious discourse	Strategy maintained	Preferred media (TV, radio, networks)
Argentina	Yes	Head of government, Minister of Health, Minister of Interior Others	No	Yes, regarding COVID First integrative, then cracks appeared	TV and networks
Bolivia	Sometimes	Head of government, Health Minister Others	War/religious	Yes President campaigning for elections	Public TV
Brazil	Yes	No	Religious	Yes – denial Two health ministers resigned	Social networks
Chile	Sometimes	Health Minister Others	War/religious	Yes Two different health ministers	TV

Table 11.2: Government communications in response to the COVID-19 crisis (continued)

Country	The President was responsible for communicating with the public	Presence of another major actor	War/religious discourse	Strategy maintained	Preferred media (TV, radio, networks)
Columbia	Yes	Health Minister Minister for Social Protection Others	No	Yes	TV, Radio and networks
Costa Rica	Sometimes	Health Minister Others	No	Yes	TV and public radio and social networks
Ecuador	No	Vice-President Government ministers Health Minister Others	War/religious	Erratic	TV, Radio and networks
El Salvador	Yes	Some ministers Armed Forces	Religious	Yes	TV, press and networks
Guatemala	Yes	Health Minister Others	Religious	Erratic Change in health minister	TV, Radio and networks

(continued)

Table 11.2: Government communications in response to the COVID-19 crisis (continued)

Country	The President was responsible for communicating with the public	Presence of another major actor	War/religious discourse	Strategy maintained	Preferred media (TV, radio, networks)
Honduras	Yes	National Risk Management System (SINAGER) Others	Religious/war	Yes	TV, Radio and networks
Mexico	No	Under-Secretary for Health	No	Yes	TV, Radio and networks
Nicaragua	No	Vice-President Others	No	Yes – denial	Public media linked to the government
Panama	Yes	Health Minister Others	Religious/war	Yes	TV, Radio and networks
Paraguay	Sometimes	Ministers	War	Yes	TV, Radio and networks
Peru	Yes	Ministers Armed Forces Others	War	Yes, first consensus, then not	TV, Radio and networks

Table 11.2: Government communications in response to the COVID-19 crisis (continued)

Country	The President was responsible for communicating with the public	Presence of another major actor	War/religious discourse	Strategy maintained	Preferred media (TV, radio, networks)
Dominican Republic	Sometimes	Minister to the Presidency, Health Minister, Candidate to the presidency	Religious	Yes, first consensus, then not	TV, Radio and networks
Uruguay	Yes	Secretary to the President and Others	No	Yes, first consensus, then not	TV, Radio and networks
Venezuela	Official: Yes Acting president: Yes	Official: Vice President and Minister for Communications Acting President: Technical experts	Official president: War/religious Acting president: No	Official: Yes Acting: Yes	Official: TV, Radio and networks Acting: networks

Source: Martí and Alcántara (2020: 372–3).

Exceptionally, however, in some countries, presidents have delegated communications to other political figures. In others, heads of state have only occasionally made an appearance because of their provisional status or because of the weight acquired by other government figures (vice-presidents, ministers of health, government and social protection), technical staff (epidemiologists, health managers, economists) or members of the armed forces. In this sense, including military personnel in the *mise-en-scène* was consistent with the construction of a patriotic discourse to which a military and, in some cases, religious discourse was added in many of the countries.

Which institution has taken the leadership role?

Once identified as communication policy, it is important to indicate which institutions and actors have assumed leadership in the crisis, noting the relevance (or not) of the head of state, the prime minister (or similar position if there is one) and the legislative or judicial authority. In order to reflect on political leadership, it is worth noting the (high, medium or low) intensity of the level of activism deployed by the president of the republic, the executive, the legislative authorities and the judiciary in each country. This task is summarized in Table 11.3.

From the data shown in Table 11.3, a recurring theme emerges: the central role of the executive, both of the head of state and of their governments. It could hardly be otherwise given the presidential nature of the region's political systems. This is reflected in the fact that presidential activism was high in almost all countries, with few exceptions. But besides the role of the president, it is worth noting that government involvement was also high, with the exceptions of Nicaragua and Bolivia.

Another very different matter is the role played by the legislative authorities or the judiciary, which was generally of medium or low intensity. Only in four countries did the legislative authority play an intense role, namely in Brazil and El Salvador, to counter the hyper-leadership of their presidents – in the case of Uruguay, due to a solid opposition and in the case of the Chilean Chamber of Deputies due to existing social mobilization. But even more lax than the legislative authority was the judiciary, which was only active in El Salvador in order to keep President Nayib Bukele in check, and in Brazil where it acted as an arbiter between institutions.

It is clear from the foregoing that the executive's involvement has been overwhelming in relation to the rest of the authorities and actors. The virtual elimination of press conferences with unscripted questions, the permanent use of direct presidential and governmental briefings to the nation and the quest to promote a presidential image have been instruments in constant use.

Has anyone objected?

After pointing out the actions taken by the authorities, it is also necessary to highlight the role played by political and social actors in the crisis, be it the opposition, the media, organized civil society or community initiatives. The positioning of actors that have supported or challenged governments, such as opposition parties, civil society, private media and community networks, also needs to be discussed. In order to assess this, Table 11.4 has been constructed to provide an overview of the level of involvement of opposition forces, the private media, social and community networks.

For a democracy to function effectively, it is important that opposition parties and the media play their part. In periods of crisis, these actors can play either an oppositional or consensus-building role and, depending on the strategy adopted, one can see how the political arena works in each country. The data shown in Table 11.4 indicate that during the COVID-19 crisis there have been countries in which the opposition – following the first few weeks after the outbreak of the pandemic – opted

Table 11.3: Institutional leadership during the COVID-19 crisis

Country	Activism/ President of the Republic	Activism/ executive	Activism/ legislative authority	Activism/ judiciary	Positive image of the President (%)*
Argentina	High	High	Medium (online)	Low	67
Bolivia	Medium	Medium	Medium Rule by decree	Low	58
Brazil	High	High	High	High Arbitrating	29
Chile	High	High	High	Low	23
Columbia	High	High	Low	Low	52
Costa Rica	Low	High	Medium	Low	50
Ecuador	Low	High	Medium	Medium	16
El Salvador	High	High	High	High	91
Guatemala	High	High	Medium	Low	64
Honduras	High	High	Medium	Low	49
Mexico	Medium	High	Low	Low	50
Nicaragua	Low	Medium	Low	Low	30
Panama	Medium	High	Medium	Low	40
Paraguay	High	High	Medium	Low	63
Peru	High	High	Low	Low	66
Dominican Republic	Low	High	Medium	Medium Central Election Board	66
Uruguay	High	High	Medium	Low	61

Table 11.3: Institutional leadership during the COVID-19 crisis (continued)

Country	Activism/ President of the Republic	Activism/ executive	Activism/ legislative authority	Activism/ judiciary	Positive image of the President (%)*
Venezuela	High	High	Low -AN Pro- government High -AN Opposition	Low	13

*The data on the presidential image are from the Legislative Directory. See: https://directoriolegislativo.org/en/informes/report-on-presidential-approval-ratings-may-jun-2020/ (Accessed 15 July 2022).

Source: Martí and Alcántara (2020: 374).

for consensus and support for the government, and others in which it maintained a strategy of confrontation, continuing with the previous dynamics that this crisis has only served to reinforce.

However, political opposition to the governments was not only experienced by the parties represented in the legislature but was often manifested from the territorial power. In countries where there has been territorial tension historically, differences have always existed between the central power and the power of large municipalities and states, provinces or departments. In some cases, these differences have stemmed from confrontations of a strictly political origin, as these entities were being governed by opposition parties. The need for some regional leaders to counterbalance the political strength of the president has much to do with their quest to improve both their own and their political parties' electoral prospects in the next elections.

On the other hand, there is the role played by the private media, which has sometimes worked intensely against the government, such as in Venezuela or Nicaragua – where the media have substituted the role of a political opposition, albeit with great limitations – or in Argentina, where confrontation

Table 11.4: Level of involvement of political and social actors in the COVID-19 crisis

Country	Role of opposition parties	Role of private media	Role of civil society organizations	Community initiatives
ARG	High	High	Medium	High
BOL	High Mayors, Department heads	High in favour	High polarization	High Mutual aid networks
BRA	High	Medium polarized	Medium	Medium
CHI	Low	Medium in favour	High Medical Association	Medium
COL	Medium	Medium in favour	Medium	Medium
CRC	Medium consensus	Medium	Medium	Medium
ECU	Medium opposition	Medium critical	High conflict	Medium
ES	Medium	Medium critical	High	Medium
GUA	Medium	Medium	Low	Low
HND	Low	Medium in favour	Medium	Low
MEX	Medium	Medium critical	Medium	Medium
NIC	Medium	High critical	High	High
PAN	Low	High	Low	Low
PGY	Medium	High	Medium	High
PE	Low	High	Low	Medium
RD	High Campaigning for elections	Medium	High	Low

Table 11.4: Level of involvement of political and social actors in the COVID-19 crisis (continued)

Country	Role of opposition parties	Role of private media	Role of civil society organizations	Community initiatives
UY	Medium	High	High	Medium
VZ	High	High opposition	High	High

Source: Martí and Alcántara, 2020: 378.

between the private mass media and *justicialismo* (the political establishment) is commonplace. In other countries, the media has strongly supported the executive, such as in Bolivia, Colombia and Honduras, as a result of the close relationship between the media system and political power, while in others, the media system has played a more diversified role – some groups being pro- and others anti-government – as has been the case in Mexico and Brazil. It should be noted that in none of the countries have the media played a minor role – as is the case with civil society, community networks or some parties – thus reflecting the fundamental role of the media in today's world. Another point to note is that in all countries without exception there has been an abundance of fake news and hoaxes circulating on social media.

The role of civil society and, of course, community initiatives should also be noted. Within this field, in Venezuela and Nicaragua, where institutional opposition is repressed, civil society actors and community initiatives have been very important and take a prominent social and political role. The case of Chile, which has seen the Chilean Medical Association play an exceptional role in managing the pandemic, also stands out. However, in most cases, civil society actors – pressure groups, trade unions, professional associations and so on – have taken on an active, though not crucial, role.

On a different note, we must not forget the ongoing presence of organized crime, as well as successive outbreaks of rioting, generally in peripheral urban areas or remote places. To this must be added the state's inability to manage certain territories over which a number of informal and illegal groups exert their control.

What kind of public policies have been promoted?

It is also important to highlight the public policies related to health, the economy and security that have been promoted to combat the COVID-19 crisis. It has been pointed out (Malamud and Núñez, 2020) that, despite their heterogeneous nature, almost all of these policies were similar and were aimed at the same goal: to prevent infections, isolate the infected and preserve the − often meagre and weak − public health systems. To this end, emphasis was placed on personal hygiene, social distancing and reducing mobility (both by monitoring and transferring incoming cases). Polymerase chain reaction testing and track-and-trace policies for the infected were also implemented, but these last two measures were less widespread due to their cost. In the end, all these measures were deployed on the basis of similar strategies (whether they were called quarantine or not). It is worth noting that these measures were adopted in 15 of the 18 countries within a minimum time frame (see Table 11.1). Likewise, in May 2020, almost all the countries started implementing very similar quarantine extension policies.

Taken together, this shows that beyond the ideology of governments and leaderships, most executives acted very similarly with regard to nominally deploying substantial policies. The most significant differences between governments were in the budget available and the state's capacity to implement the measures in question. The question needs to be asked of how it was possible that governments so different from one another could have implemented such similar policies.

The most plausible answer is not that convergence in policy decision-making has resulted from reflection on best possible practice, nor from a unilateral imposition, but because policies implemented in some countries have been taken as a reference, thus influencing the decisions of others and resulting in the same measures being adopted (Meseguer and Gilardi, 2008).

Another aspect that deserves attention is the effectiveness of such measures on a country-by-country basis. And this – in addition to 'government will and capacity' – has depended on structural factors, such as investment in the health sector and 'stateness', and also on certain conditions, such as population density, the level of informal employment and the relative isolation of the country (Martí and Alcántara, 2020). In this sense, the pandemic has 'understood' very little about ideologies and charismatic leaders. Yet, one can see that the worst strategy was to deny reality, which was the tactic chosen by President Jair Bolsonaro in Brazil.

Latin American democracies after the pandemic: weary or sick?

The political situation in the aftermath of the COVID-19 crisis is not promising, adding to the deterioration experienced during the previous decade by democratic regimes. A lack of trust in politics, the assumption that democracy 'does not solve problems' and the perception that corruption has not abated have clearly led to a situation characterized not only by difficulties in representation but also by acute polarization (Alcántara, 2020a, 2020b). The electoral dynamic itself, which had worked reasonably well in recent years, has begun to show weaknesses in its functioning, as highlighted by the recent elections in Venezuela, Nicaragua, Honduras and Paraguay. Meanwhile, the existence of political dynamics with strong, personality-driven presidencies in Brazil, Mexico and El Salvador could lead to democratic erosion. Moreover, in countries such as Argentina, Colombia, Chile or Ecuador, the discontent seen on the streets is a sign of a new cycle of tension and instability.

At the same time, various indicators measuring the quality of democracy over the last five years (V-Dem, The Economist Intelligence Unit, the Bertelsmann Transformation Index) have revealed that it has been deteriorating in recent years. The concentration of power in the hands of presidents for handling extraordinary measures to tackle the pandemic, together with restrictions on rights, may serve to maintain the inertia in favour of strong governments. To this must be added a backlog of unresolved problems, which are likely to be exacerbated by the pandemic and its aftermath. The risk of the difficult circumstances described here lies in the potential for authoritarianism that leaders may have been able to deploy during the months of the pandemic, when the activism of many leaders has been noteworthy (Alcántara, 2020c). Moreover, the combination of the effects of the economic crisis with the emptying of state coffers and the decline in representation has led to the strengthening or upsurge of proposals that have an authoritarian bias in the purest tradition of the region – although cases such as that of Chile seem to be moving in the opposite direction.

The problem in the face of future uncertainty is that often, when things get complicated, it is easy to revert to traditional formulas, and in Latin America, messianic *caudillismo* (political domination) and populism are just such formulae. Thus, in the democratic arena, Latin America's governments are facing the toughest test of the last 30–40 years (Meléndez, 2020; Reid, 2020; Rodríguez and Ivarez, 2020). It is clear that the political cycle following the outbreak of the COVID-19 pandemic will have a significant impact on the region's democracies and will be further exacerbated by the handling of vaccine policies. There are five aspects of the political fallout from the health crisis that stand out:

• The pre-eminence of the executive branch over all other institutions.

- The personalization of politics to the detriment of parties.
- The judicialization of politics as a tool to oppose those in power.
- The (even) greater importance of mass media, both traditional media and social networks.
- And increasing distrust in the work of politicians among the general public.

These aspects imply the concentration of power in few institutions and few hands, as well as greater intra-institutional and media conflict and a strong erosion of social capital. In this sense, it can be said that the critical situation resulting from the COVID-19 crisis has generated less polyarchic systems, which are under greater tension. In these circumstances, the danger lies in a possible decline in democratic principles that – although it already existed before the pandemic – could increase. In the case of the opening of an illiberal cycle, it could be affirmed that the COVID-19 crisis has had effects similar to the stock market crash in 1929, the oil crisis of 1973 and the debt crisis of 1982. Nevertheless, it remains to be seen whether, after the first cycle of the health crisis, marked by public emergency, exceptional circumstances and political personalization, a new period is to come requiring a political logic more focused on the administrative and managerial capacity of the state to meet the challenge of vaccine rollout and economic recovery.

Note

[1]   See www.worldometers.info/coronavirus

References

Alcántara Sáez, M. (2020a) 'América Latina vota (2017–19): elecciones en el marco de una democracia fatigada', in M. Alcántara (ed) *América Latina Vota*, 2017–2019, Madrid: Tecnos.

Alcántara Sáez, M. (2020b) 'Del alboroto al silencio: la política en tiempos de incertidumbre', *Metapolítica*, 109 (April–June): 20–7.

Alcántara Sáez, M. (2020c) 'América Latina ante la "nueva normalidad"', *Política Exterior* (July–August): 88–98.

Mahoney, J. (2000) 'Path dependence in historical sociology', *Theory and Society*, 29(4): 507–48.

Malamud, C. and Núñez, R. (2020) 'América Latina: del exitismo al pico de la pandemia', Informe del Real Instituto Elcano, ARI 79/2020. Available from: http://www.realinstitutoelcano.org/wps/portal/rielcano_es/contenido?WCM_GLOBAL_CONTEXT=/elcano/elcano_es/zonas_es/ari79-malamud-nunez-america-latina-del-exitismo-al-pico-de-la-pandemia

Martí I Puig, S. and Alcántara, M. (eds) (2020) 'Política y crisis en América Latina: Reacción e impacto frente a la covid-19', Madrid: Cátedra de Cultura Jurídica Marcial Pons.

Meléndez, C. (2020) 'Crisis política en Perú V: elecciones en tiempos de política post-partidaria', Cipher Chile, 20 November. Available from: https://www.ciperchile.cl/2020/11/20/crisis-politica-en-peru-v-elecciones-en-tiempos-de-politica-post-partidaria

Meseguer, C. and Gilardi, F. (2008) 'Reflexiones sobre el debate de la difusión de políticas', *Política y gobierno*, 15(2): 315–51.

Reid, M. (2020) 'América Latina entre el virus y la calle', *Política Exterior* (July–August): 100–10.

Rodríguez, É. and Álvarez, A. (2020) 'El impacto de la COVID-19 en América Latina: situación a nivel sanitario, político y económico', in E. Rodríguez (ed), *Informe Iberoamérica: América Latina ante la protesta y la pandemia*, Madrid: Fundación Alternativas, 115–35.

TWELVE

Vietnam's Response to the COVID-19 Pandemic

Edward Lahiff, Pham Quang Minh and Nguyễn Trọng Chính

Vietnam is a middle-income country in South East Asia, with a population of 97 million people, that has experienced rapid urbanization, industrialization and socioeconomic development since the late 1980s.[1] The health profile of the population is generally high, by international standards, and its health sector is considered to be well developed and effective. Vietnam is a one-party state under the leadership of the Communist Party of Vietnam, with a strong central government but also with many powers delegated to its 58 provinces and five major municipalities. The country has a thriving economy with an extensive private sector and has, in recent decades, attracted high volumes of foreign investment and been progressively integrated into global markets.

The first case of COVID-19 in Vietnam was reported on 23 January 2020. The government responded swiftly through rapid testing, contact tracing, quarantine and social distancing measures. As a result, case numbers throughout 2020 were limited to levels that were remarkably low by international standards. Extensive economic supports were provided to companies forced to suspend operations and to workers who lost employment, although gaps in coverage were widely reported. By May 2020, many restrictions had been lifted, and society and economy were beginning to return to normal. The mobilization of all aspects of state and society, in a spirit of patriotism, is generally seen as the decisive factor in Vietnam's success in combatting the first waves of the pandemic, saving lives and limiting socioeconomic disruption (World Bank, 2020: xi).

In mid-2021, however, Vietnam was hit by a further – fourth – wave of the COVID-19 infection, this time driven largely by the Delta variant, which proved much more severe in terms of infection and deaths, as well as its economic impact. Again, this was met with a comprehensive state response, which, at the time of writing in 2022, is being gradually scaled back.

This chapter traces the course of the COVID-19 pandemic in Vietnam and the response from state and society. The very different experiences of the first and fourth waves raise many questions, which are the subject of ongoing debate.

The spread of COVID-19 in 2020 and the response of the state and society

Following the first reported cases in February 2020, the government responded quickly, with a well-coordinated, comprehensive and highly effective approach involving mass mobilization of health workers, state officials, security services and social partners, effective public communications, widespread testing, contract tracing and quarantining, treatment of infected persons and curtailment of international travel. Within a week, a National COVID Steering Committee, chaired by a deputy prime minister, was established that met every two days to coordinate the country's 'whole of government' strategy. On 1 February, the outbreak was declared an epidemic (Nguyen et al, 2020), and a pandemic from 1 April 2020. From the initial outbreak, the government of Vietnam rapidly accelerated efforts to contain the spread of the virus and provide treatment for those infected, with a focus on social distancing, including closures of schools and other non-essential facilities, as well as isolation, quarantine and travel restrictions. One of the reasons widely mentioned for Vietnam's ability to react so quickly to the pandemic and to keep the case count so low in 2020 was the country's experience of a severe acute respiratory syndrome epidemic in 2003 and human cases of avian influenza between 2004 and 2010.

The state took a targeted approach to testing, scaling it up in areas with community transmission, aggressively tracing and isolating contacts of infected persons as well as their contacts, along with dramatic restrictions on economic and social activity (Le et al, 2021). Contact tracing involved three degrees of contacts for each positive case. As a result, hundreds of thousands of people, including international travellers and those in close contact with people who tested positive, were placed in official quarantine centres for 14 days, proving highly effective in restricting transmission (Pollack et al, 2021). A second wave of cases was identified in early March, and the government moved quickly to track and isolate about 200 close contacts of those infected. A third wave was reported in the city of Da Nang in July and August 2020, leading to an immediate city-wide lockdown.

The National Response Plan provided detailed plans across all sectors for controlling the spread of the virus, with the slogan 'each citizen is a warrior to fight COVID-19' (ILO, 2020: 10). Strict social distancing rules were applied nationwide for an initial period of 15 days, later extended to 21 days or more in 12 provinces considered to be higher risk, including self-isolation and restrictions on people from leaving homes except for food and medicines. The gathering of more than two people was banned, and everyone was required to maintain a distance of two meters when outdoors. Social distancing measures were loosened in many areas from 23 April 2020 to allow businesses to reopen, but cross-border movement remained largely restricted. Lower and higher secondary schools nationwide remained closed until 4 May 2020 and primary schools until 11 May (UNICEF, 2020: 6).

By 25 July, Vietnam had confirmed just 270 cases in total, despite extensive testing, and no community transmission since 15 April – a remarkable 99 days. By 8 September, 551 locally transmitted cases were reported from 15 cities and provinces across the country, with Da Nang and nearby Quang Nam province most affected. Again, Vietnam turned to the strategies that had been successful in ending earlier outbreaks: targeted lockdowns, travel bans, business closures, mass quarantining and widespread testing (Pollack et al, 2021). By September, the economy was slowly returning to a 'new normal', although international travel continued to be restricted.

As in other countries, the economic impact of COVID-19 in Vietnam and the measures taken to control it were severe (World Bank, 2020: xii). Retail, transportation, personal services and tourism, along with manufacturing, were hit hard, with major falls in employment and earnings reported. Manufacturing was further hit by disruption to supply chains and a slowdown in global demand. Initial social distancing measures had an immediate effect on informal workers such as street vendors, scrap vendors, garbage collectors and informal motorbike taxi drivers (CDI, 2021: 11). Unemployment rose to the highest rate in 10 years: 2.4 million workers were reported to have lost their jobs, and as many as 17.6 million were believed to have had their income affected (ILO, 2020: 7). Among the worst affected were migrants from the rural areas, unskilled workers and those employed in the informal sector (United Nations Vietnam, 2020: 8). According to a survey by Oxfam (2020) carried out in March 2020, the most vulnerable groups identified were labourers without a contract and migrant workers – including waste collectors, domestic workers, street vendors, unlicensed small businesses, motorbike taxi and taxi drivers, porters at wholesale markets and other workers in the service sector.

The government of Vietnam introduced a comprehensive package of support for businesses, workers and vulnerable groups affected by the shutdown, including extending deadlines for payment of taxes (World Bank, 2020: xii; Tran et al, 2021: 9). On 9 April, the government issued Resolution no. 42 / NQ-CP on measures to support people in difficulties due to the COVID-19 pandemic, with a financial package worth VND 62 trillion (approximately US$2.6 billion; VND = Vietnamese dong [đồng]. One US dollar was worth approximately VND 24,000 at this time) (ILO, 2020: 12). Payment of VND 1.8 million per month was available to employees whose labour contract was temporarily suspended or who had to take unpaid leave, while VND 1 million per month (about US $43) was provided to those workers who were not eligible for unemployment allowance (World Bank, 2021: 34). While many categories of workers benefitted, there were widespread reports of migrants and informal sector workers facing bureaucratic delays and struggling to obtain support payments (United Nations Vietnam, 2020: 11). Street vendors, in particular, were badly hit during the nationwide lockdown in April 2020 (CARE, 2020: 13).

In January 2021, the Center for Development and Integration documented a wide range of support services from an array of state, party and civil society organizations that had provided support to workers and vulnerable groups affected by COVID-19, including trade unions, business organizations and mass organizations such as the Vietnam Fatherland Front and the Vietnam Women's Union (CDI, 2021: 31–5). 'Rice ATMs', dispensing free rice to the population, was one of many innovative solutions. A different situation was found outside the major urban areas. United Nations Vietnam (2020: 9) reported that millions of rural households fell outside of the government's cash assistance package and suffered severe decreases in household income as a direct result of the pandemic, exacerbated by increased food prices and loss of school meals for children due to school closures.

By March 2021, the country had recorded just 2,567 confirmed cases and 35 deaths and appeared to have weathered the worst of the pandemic. Most sectors of the economy had returned to pre-pandemic levels of operation, and social distancing measures had been relaxed throughout the country. Many commentators attributed the successes of this period to a spirit of patriotism and solidarity rooted in Vietnam's struggles for independence, captured in the widely used slogan 'no one left behind'. While the public health measures adopted by the government had proved highly effective, a programme of mass vaccination had yet to start.

2021: the fourth wave

Despite signs of optimism and of a return to near-normal conditions, there were worrying signs throughout the early months of 2021, particularly around the slow rollout of vaccines. Rising case numbers of COVID-19 were being reported, and April 2021 is now seen as the beginning of Vietnam's fourth wave. After some trials, the government launched Phase 1 of the vaccination campaign on 8 March 2021, focusing on the frontline workers. As of 25 April, a total of 209,632 doses of vaccines had been administered, but it was September before 1 million people were fully vaccinated (WHO, 2021: 1). Vietnam was slow to move on bilateral arrangements for the purchase of vaccines, relying instead on the global COVAX programme, coordinated by the World Health Organization (WHO) and its partners and donations from countries such as China and the United States. In July, the country purchased 2 million doses of the AstraZeneca vaccine, and negotiations were underway to buy supplies of Pfizer-BioNTech's vaccine. The vaccination numbers accelerated rapidly through September and October 2021, and by 6 November 32.1 million had received at least one dose and 28.8 were fully vaccinated, equivalent to 29.8 per cent of the total population (VN Express, 2021). This was well behind other countries in the region, such as Indonesia and the Philippines.

Infection rates started rising significantly from early July and reached a peak of almost 15,000 daily infections on 3 September (with a second, lesser wave being reported in October–November), overwhelming the health services – and especially the acute hospitals – in many areas. The army was deployed to restrict movement and deliver food and other goods to residents under lockdown. Hanoi was divided into red, orange and green zones, based on infection risk, with differing degrees of restrictions. Mass testing was carried out in Ho Chi Minh City and Hanoi. Daily death numbers peaked at 440 on 31 August, being heavily concentrated in Ho Chi Minh City, where deaths exceeded 200 a day (Reuters, 2021a). As of 12 November, Vietnam had exceeded a total of 1 million infections and 22,849 COVID-related deaths since the pandemic began.

During this fourth wave, restrictions were gradually tightened across the country, and Ho Chi Minh City re-established COVID-19 checkpoints at the entrances of the city from 15 May. By the end of the month, specific districts in the city were under severe lockdown under government Directive 15. Restrictions were extended throughout the Mekong Delta region in July, including night-time curfews. Hanoi, which had opened up many services in May, began to reimpose a lockdown in July, including quarantine for travellers arriving from southern provinces. The most severe lockdowns were imposed in August, with authorities in Ho Chi Minh City applying the strict 'shelter-in-place' lockdown restrictions until 15 September and bringing with it massive disruption to economic activity. Tight rules were imposed on factories from early July, effectively forcing companies to choose between housing and feeding workers in 'manufacturing bubbles' or shutting down. Factories around Ho Chi Minh City were required to implement a 'three-on-site' policy, which meant workers would eat, sleep and work on-site, or the 'one route-two destinations policy' whereby workers were transported from their residence or dormitory by company vehicles to the worksite (Vietnamnet, 2021). The city introduced a 'green card' system giving greater freedom to operate normally for companies whose staff have received two vaccine doses. Residents were not allowed to leave their homes even for food, instead relying on deliveries, and then only for goods deemed essential. On 23 August 2021, troops were again deployed in Ho Chi Minh City to tighten the lockdown under a new, and more severe, Directive 16. Throughout the country, citizens complained of rapid rises in prices of food and other essential goods.

As in the previous year, the government of Vietnam responded to the fourth wave with an extensive support package, in terms of Resolution 68/NQCP of 1 July 2021, worth VND 26 trillion, and operating under the slogan 'Ensuring social protection and promoting economic recovery, production and business stabilization' (UNDP, 2021: 1). In October, under Decision no. 28/2021/QD-TTg, a further allocation of VND 38 trillion was provided to support workers eligible for unemployment insurance (Ministry of Construction, 2021). In a comprehensive analysis, UNDP (2021: 2) argued that this second package fell short of meeting the needs of people and enterprises affected by the COVID-19 fourth wave, with the great majority of survey respondents having received no financial support. The financial package was found to rely too much on suspension of social insurance and other contributions, rather than direct cash support to vulnerable groups and depended too much on local budgets, leading to much inefficiency and inequality between provinces. Migrants were again singled out as particularly vulnerable, often being denied any assistance due to their temporary residence status in areas where they worked (UNDP, 2021: 5).

Efforts by the state were matched by an extraordinary effort by broader society (Ha et al, 2021). Support for Ho Chi Minh City was compared to the support of the North for South Vietnam during the struggle against the United

States, with the slogan 'All for our beloved Southern region'. Health professionals and other volunteers, as well as material support, came to the city from across the country in a spirit of community solidarity, a key value of Vietnamese society, much promoted by the government and other institutions at the time. There is general agreement that the social and economic impacts of the fourth wave far exceeded the effects in 2020, and the economic growth that had been maintained in 2020 – against the global trend – was largely reversed in 2021. Vietnam's gross domestic product dropped by 6.17 per cent for the year for the July–September period, the first quarterly decline since 2000 (Reuters, 2021b). The third quarter underperformed even more than the second quarter of 2020, with just 0.39 per cent growth being reported.

In late September, the government acknowledged that Vietnam could no longer pursue a zero-COVID strategy and would instead pursue a 'new normal' policy of aiming to contain the disease. On 11 October, the government adopted Resolution 128/NQ-CP on 'Safe, flexible and effective control of COVID-19 outbreak', which sought to protect people's lives, mitigate fatalities and map out recovery plans in pursuit of the goal of containing the virus while developing the economy. The gradual reopening of economy and society brought with it a further upward trend in infections and deaths from late November to early February 2022; while infections were up, deaths were well below the figures witnessed in August (WHO, 2022).

2022: Omicron, mass vaccination and an end in sight?

In 2022, the Omicron variant helped drive the single biggest wave of infections, running from early February to early April 2022. The first case of the Omicron variant of concern was reported on 27 December 2021, in a traveller coming from the UK, and the first cases of community transmission were being detected throughout the country by late January (WHO, 2022).

Cities such as Hanoi and Da Nang imposed restrictions on mass events during Tet holidays; public health measures such as mask wearing remained in place, but internal movement was not restricted. Total daily infections rose rapidly, reaching a peak in mid–March, but again death rates were much lower than in the previous wave. By late April, the WHO was reporting an overall downward trend in daily cases, severe cases and deaths nationwide, and no longer found evidence of strain on the healthcare system; daily deaths dipped below ten per day. The cumulative totals, however, were stark: 10,563,502 confirmed cases and 43,004 deaths were reported as of 24 April 2022 (WHO, 2022).

As in other countries, the impact of the Omicron wave was greatly tempered by the success of Vietnam's mass vaccination campaign, which started in March 2021. By 24 April 2022, over 212 million doses had been administered, using nine different vaccines; first and second shots had been administered to over 80 per cent of the population, and over 15 million people had received booster or further doses (WHO, 2022). In March 2022, the Ministry of Health introduced vaccinations for children aged five to 11 years and, by April was planning to extend this to children aged three and four years of age (Ministry of Health, 2022).

Despite the Omicron wave, Vietnam proceeded to gradually reopen the country and the economy, with only minor local setbacks. International flights between Vietnam and nine destinations were recommenced from 1 January 2022. On 18 January, the government issued a directive allowing foreign employees and overseas Vietnamese with valid tests and visa exemption certificates to enter the country (Vietnam Briefing, 2022). By mid–March, Vietnam had reopened for international tourism, with visitors only being required to test negative for the virus prior to arrival (Vietnam Plus, 2022). By the beginning of April, virtually all workplaces, schools, bars and restaurants were fully reopened, with the only requirement being the wearing of masks in indoor settings, and the country was preparing to welcome athletes from around the region to the 31st South East Asian Games.

As outlined in this chapter, the COVID-19 pandemic in Vietnam has fallen into three main phases. The first phase, covering much of 2020, saw a highly coordinated, multi-actor and multi-sector response, led by central government, that was extraordinarily effective in minimizing infection rates and deaths. This success has been widely attributed to the preparedness of the Vietnamese health system following the experience of previous pandemics, particularly in areas of testing and contact tracing and the ability of the state to make key public health decisions rapidly and implement them across the national territory. In doing so, the state invoked the spirit of national pride and resilience that characterized previous struggles of the Vietnamese people, which was met in turn by widespread support from the business sector and civil society organizations, and a high degree of compliance by citizens. A substantial financial package to businesses and individuals greatly cushioned the economic impact, although the evidence suggests that many vulnerable groups, including migrants and informal workers, missed out on support measures and were severely affected as a result.

The contrasting experience of 2021, and particularly the so-called fourth wave driven by the Delta variant, raised many questions about the assumed successes of the first wave in 2020. It is still too early to pinpoint what factors led to such a dramatic and deadly wave in 2021, and few authors have yet attempted such an analysis. There is little evidence either in contemporary debates or subsequent analysis to suggest that public health controls were relaxed too soon or too rapidly, or that an unreasonable degree of complacency took hold of either government or the general population. The stand-out factor – highlighted by virtually all commentators – is the very late, and initially slow, rollout of mass vaccination. Vietnam was not alone among countries of the Global South in struggling to acquire vaccines in the early months of the pandemic.

Limited efforts were made by government to procure vaccines on the global market, which instead relied on the COVAX programme and donations from other countries. The initial emphasis on vaccination of health professionals and other frontline workers was entirely appropriate, but the subsequent rollout to the general population was undoubtedly slow. The much greater transmissibility of the Delta variant appears – despite international warnings – to have taken many in Vietnam by surprise and, once established within the community, spread with frightening rapidity and quickly overwhelmed public health and clinical services, especially in the big cities.

The Omicron wave, from early 2022, provides yet another, more positive, contrast. Despite very high rates of infection, deaths were relatively limited, the public health system was not overwhelmed as it had been under Delta and the economy and society were not subjected to a repeat of the massive disruptions of the previous years. A key component of this has been the success of the national vaccination campaign, which, from a relatively slow start, has reached one of the highest rates of population coverage in the world.

The lessons of the COVID-19 pandemic are currently being applied in Vietnam. In August 2021, the government established a Working Group on Vaccine Diplomacy, which the Minister of Foreign Affairs, Bui Thanh Son, described as 'very important and urgent', and which has since proven its worth in terms of vaccine procurement (Vietnam Plus, 2021). Further evidence of a desire to enhance health cooperation with international partners can be seen in the establishment in August, by the US authorities, of the Southeast Asia Center for Disease Control and Prevention in Hanoi. Debate continues around the effectiveness of public communication strategies, which, in the early waves, appeared to be highly effective, but were less so in overcoming vaccine hesitancy among the public in 2021. Expansion of the network of public hospitals and recruitment of many additional health professionals are being pursued as part of building a more resilient health system in the country. Existing inequalities facing informal workers, migrants and other marginalized groups were highlighted, and even exacerbated, by the pandemic, suggesting that Vietnam faces ongoing challenges in creating a truly inclusive society and economy. At the time of writing (April 2022), it would appear that Vietnam has weathered the worst of the COVID storm and, despite huge costs in terms of mortality, morbidity and socioeconomic disruptions, has achieved success with disease control and vaccination in line with international standards and is emerging from the pandemic with a stronger and more resilient public health system.

Note

[1]   The authors gratefully acknowledge financial support from Irish Aid and the Irish Research Council under the 'Coalesce' programme.

References

CARE International (2020) 'Rapid gender analysis for COVID-19'. CARE Vietnam, May. Available from: https://www.care.org.vn/wp-content/uploads/2020/06/Viet-Nam-RGA-report_final.pdf

Center for Development and Integration (CDI) (2021) 'Initiatives on social protection: supporting Vietnamese workers in response to COVID-19', Hanoi: CDI. Available from: http://cdivietnam.org/wp-content/uploads/2021/04/210322_Intiatives-supporting-workers-in-Covid_Eng.pdf

Ha, B.T.T., La, N.Q., Thanh, P.Q., Duc, D.M., Mirzoev, T. and Bui, M.A. (2021) 'Community engagement in the prevention and control of COVID-19: insights from Vietnam', PLOS One, 8 September. Available from: https://doi.org/10.1371/journal.pone.0254432

ILO (2020) 'COVID-19 situation – impacts and responses: what trade unions and employers need to know', Special Edition Bulletin, ILO. Available from: https://www.ilo.org/hanoi/Whatwedo/Publications/WCMS_744705/lang--en/index.htm

Le, T.-A.T., Vodden, K., Wu, J. and Atiwesh, G. (2021) 'Policy responses to the COVID-19 pandemic in Vietnam', *International Journal of Environmental Research and Public Health*, 18: 559. Available from: https://doi.org/10.3390/ijerph18020559

Ministry of Construction (Vietnam) (2021) 'Localities, sectors nationwide ready for the new normal', Press Release, 13 October. Available from: https://moc.gov.vn/en/news/69132/localities-sectors-nationwide-ready-for-the-new-normal.aspx

Ministry of Health, Vietnam (2022) 'Portal of the Ministry of Health on the position of COVID-19'. Available from: https://covid19.gov.vn

Nguyen N.H., Van Nguyen T., Nguyen A.Q., Van Nguyen P. and Nguyen T.N.M. (2020) 'The first cohort of the COVID-19 patients in Vietnam and the national response to the pandemic', *Int J Med Science*, 17(16): 2449–53. Available from: https://www.medsci.org/v17p2449

Oxfam (2020) 'Leaving no one behind'. Available from: https://vietnam.oxfam.org/latest/stories/leaving-no-one-behind

Pollack, T., Thwaites, G., Rabaa, M., Choisy, M., van Doorn, R., Tan, L.V. et al (2021) 'Emerging COVID-19 success story: Vietnam's commitment to containment', Exemplars in Global Health and Our World in Data. Available from: https://ourworldindata.org/covid-exemplar-vietnam#licence

Reuters (2021a) 'COV1D-19 tracker: Vietnam'. Available from: https://graphics.reuters.com/world-coronavirus-tracker-and-maps/countries-and-territories/vietnam

Reuters (2021b) 'Vietnam posts record GDP slump in Q3 due to COVID-19 curbs'. Available from: https://www.reuters.com/world/asia-pacific/vietnam-posts-record-gdp-slump-q3-due-covid-19-curbs-2021-09-29/

Tran, T.P.T., Le, T.H., Nguyen, T.N.P. and Hoang, V.M. (2021) 'Rapid response to the COVID-19 pandemic: Vietnam government's experience and preliminary success', *Journal of Global Health*, 10(2) (6 April): 020502.

UNICEF (2020) 'Rapid assessment on the social and economic impacts of Covid-19 on children and families in Viet Nam', Hanoi: UNICEF, August. Available from: https://www.unicef.org/vietnam/reports/rapid-assessment-social-and-economic-impacts-covid-19-children-and-families-viet-nam

UNDP (2021) 'Rapid assessment of the design and implementation of government's 2nd support package for people affected by Covid-19: summary report', Hanoi: United Nations Development Programme, September. Available from: https://www.vn.undp.org/content/dam/vietnam/docs/Publications/UNDP_Baocao Covid_DungN-24-9-2021-Eng.pdf

United Nations Vietnam (2020) 'UN analysis on social impacts of Covid-19 and strategic policy recommendations for Viet Nam', Hanoi: United Nations. Available from: https://www.unicef.org/vietnam/media/5996/file/UN%20analysis%20on%20social%20impacts%20of%20COVID-19%20and%20strategic%20policy%20recommendations%20for%20Viet%20Nam.pdf

Vietnam Briefing (2022) 'Dezan Shira & Associates'. Available from: https://www.vietnam-briefing.com/news/vietnam-business-operations-and-the-coronavirus-updates.html

Vietnamnet (2021) '"3 on-site" model runs into problems as virus spreads inside facilities'. Available from: https://vietnamnet.vn/en/business/3-on-site-model-runs-into-problems-as-virus-spreads-inside-isolated-facilities-764866.html

Vietnam Plus (2021) 'Vaccine diplomacy is very important and urgent: minister', 8 September. Available from: https://en.vietnamplus.vn/vaccine-diplomacy-is-very-important-and-urgent-minister/207679.vnp

Vietnam Plus (2022), 'Vietnam fully reopens borders to tourists', 15 March. Available from: https://en.vietnamplus.vn/vietnam-fully-reopens-borders-to-tourists/223538.vnp

VN Express (2021) 'Covid-19 in Vietnam: vaccination data'. Available from: https://e.vnexpress.net/covid-19/vaccine

VNP (2021) 'Viet Nam may approve at least one domestic COVID-19 vaccine this year', 14 September. Available from: http://news.chinhphu.vn/Home/Viet-Nam-may-approve-at-least-one-domestic-COVID19-vaccine-this-year/20219/45478.vgp

World Bank (2020) 'Taking stock, July 2020: what will be the new normal for Vietnam? The economic impact of COVID-19', Washington, DC: World Bank Group. Available from: https://openknowledge.worldbank.org/handle/10986/34268

World Bank (2021) 'The labor market and the COVID-19 outbreak in Vietnam: impacts and lessons learned for social protection', Washington, DC: World Bank Group. Available from: https://openknowledge.worldbank.org/handle/10986/35990

WHO (2021) 'Viet Nam COVID-19 situation report #39', 25 April, Vietnam: WHO. Available from: https://www.who.int/docs/default-source/wpro---documents/countries/viet-nam/covid-19/viet-nam-moh-who-covid-19-sitrep_25apr2021.pdf?sfvrsn=512b518e_5&download=true

WHO (2022) 'Viet Nam COVID-19 situation report #90', 24 April 2022. Available from: https://www.who.int/vietnam/internal-publications-detail/covid-19-in-viet-nam-situation-report-90

Conclusion

Ashok Acharya

For most of us lucky enough to have survived, the pandemic has been – and remains – a once-in-a-lifetime experience. For the few of us adept at using social science lenses, the implications of the pandemic have been grave, profound and diverse. With the threat of further waves looming and inequity still causing unnecessary suffering, we are yet to see the end of this crisis. Into its third year, the long-term effects of this pandemic are visible on many fronts. The global economy has taken a big hit, governance is under new pressures, access to health resources continues to be a severe challenge and new social fault lines overlapping the old social injustices have emerged around the world. To make matters worse, the pandemic struck us at a time when in the backdrop global inequality has been on the rise, collective action issues, ranging from climate change to global trade and migration, have remained unresolved, and democratic backsliding, war and regression have been on the upswing.

The past two years and more have been some of the most momentous in modern human history. The health crisis that arrived with the COVID-19 pandemic has scarred society around the world and continues to bring up unexpected and formidable challenges for governments and civil society alike. With the relentless struggle against climate change and rolling conflicts across the Sahel, the Middle East and Eastern Europe already impacting heavily on human development in just about every region on earth, the pandemic has brought forward another, albeit anticipated, crisis for us all. What it has revealed has been an existential realization that all humanity is vulnerable to this type of viral contagion. Through the responsive actions to combat COVID-19 there has also been the revelation that investment in health and the use of public resources have not been effectively or efficiently balanced to give populations equitable sustainable human development.

The risks that the pandemic have exposed have been a hard lesson for us all and, as we have seen, have intensified the cyclical nature of underdevelopment and the further diversification of life experiences on a global scale. Essentially and increasingly, the gap between the two worlds of those 'that have' and those that 'have not' has been forced to the extreme. It can be seen in terms of survival and mortality, but also conversely in terms of levels of life enhancing society and connectivity – that is, how well we can cope with systemic adversity, what we can source in terms of healthcare and sustenance, rights and a basic quality of life and livelihood. All of this came into play as the patterns of mitigation affected our respective societies on a global scale. This noted, there are also the positive responses that can be seen throughout this time: the heroic role of civil society, the governments who against the odds have risen to protect their people, the good people who stepped forward as health and care workers to help the sick and dying, and the communities who garnered solidarity to work their way through such adversity. They all need to be celebrated.

The approach taken in this book gives insight into how various parts of the world and indeed institutional and social sectors responded to this crisis. Its scope and range provide an overview of where the Global South is in a third year of the pandemic. With this, it presents answers to a number of questions. First, it serves as a review of the first two years of the pandemic and how this affected some of the most vulnerable people and communities, showing how different countries reacted and revealing how different responses took effect around the world. Indeed, it provides a space to profile successes in the Global South as well as highlighting the global injustices. Second, it looked at the responses in local terms in the Global South, highlighting, for example, how communities dealt with such a traumatic event 'from below'. Third, it offers pathways to recovery: how the complexities of our global community can rebuild and renew its humanity. Finally, it suggests a reckoning, a reconstruction of relationships on a global scale that will prepare us for the next, and sadly inevitable, pandemic. Beyond these general observations, some salient and more targeted points jump out from this book.

- That there is a need to decommodify life-saving medication, making the process from development, through procurement to distribution and administering, not-for-profit and universally available.
- Health services globally should be definancialized and healthcare free at the point of need. Care and health provision remain a fundamental right that should not be compromised or subjected to the failings and inequality that comes with market forces.
- Crucially, that politicians should act as servants of the people, working for the protection of all their people. It brings us back to a culture of public service that makes the profession a privilege for those involved and not, as is the case in many countries, the entitlement of an elite.
- Global inequality in all its destructive guises needs to be dealt with as a defence against necropolitics, the wanton disregard of the lives of the weakest and most marginalized sectors of societies.
- Global resources need to be more equitably shared, particularly medical resources and services. There is a demand to position the health sector globally as the key to development. Everything else follows. This seems to be one of the biggest lessons from this pandemic.
- Corporate greed, tax avoidance and monopolies urgently need to be monitored, regulated and controlled, and governmental responsibility in this regard should be paramount.

- Corporate social responsibility could be legislated for globally.
- Civil society and community-based initiatives have been seen to be life-saving during the pandemic in all contexts and should be supported as a second arm of public service. The volunteers, the women's groups, the youth groups, the legions of people who stepped forward to keep communities running and safe in a myriad of ways should be recognized for their role in society.
- Human rights-based approaches enhance social and political resilience and remain the capstone of democratic life.
- Finally, and among other things that can be taken from this book, global interdependence between peoples, governments, economies and civil society, particularly in times of profound crisis such as this, should be recognized as a central plank of human development.

With all this noted, the role of global institutions such as the World Health Organization, the United Nations, the US Centers for Disease Control and Prevention and international financial institutions, among others, gives them a unique position to coordinate the rebalancing of global forces, services and resources to construct a sustainable recovery process. Given the billions of people who have been afflicted by this pandemic, the millions who have lost their lives and the countless livelihoods ruined, and the mixed, often confused, governmental responses, it demands a concerted response similar to the reconstruction plans that brought countries beyond the world at war. Ordinary people have of course their role to play, but governments collectively and individually have the primary responsibility for life-enhancing recovery and coordinating preparations for the next global crisis.

Index

Page numbers in *italic* type refer to figures.
Reference to endnotes show both the
page number and the note number (231n3).

A

Access to COVID-19 Tools
   (ACT) 61
Accredited Service Health Activists
   (ASHA) 135–6, 143
activism 78, 80–6, 88–90, 170,
   172, 178
Africa 38–47, 51, 52n1, 56, 59,
   61, *62*, 66, 153, 157
   see also individual countries,
   Sub-Saharan African
Africa Centres for Disease Control
   and Prevention (Africa
   CDC) 52n1, 66
Africa Vaccine Acquisitions Trust
   (AVAT) 66
AIDS 14, 68
   see also HIV
Amnesty International 27, 65, 97
Anganwadi Workers (AWW) 135,
   136, 143
Angola 46, 48, 51
anxiety 2, 10, 118
Argentina 61, 164, 166, 172–3,
   177
AstraZeneca 58–61, 64–5, 97, 186
austerity 26, 28, 41
Australia 58
authoritarianism 10, 15, 16, 178
avian flu 12, 183

B

Bertelsmann Transformation
   Index 178
Bezos, Jeff 26
big data 12

Bill & Melinda Gates
   Foundation 60
billionaires 26, 108
BioNTech 58, 65, 107, 122, 186
biotechnology 44
blowback 104–5, 113, 114
Bolivia 164, 166, 170, 172, 175
Bolsonaro, Jair 11, 14–16, 18,
   177
Brazil 9–10, 13–18, 27, 60–1,
   163, 164, 166, 171–7
   see also Bolsonaro, Jair, Sistema
   Único de Saúde (SUS)
Brexit 106

C

Canada 58
cancer 93–6, 101n1
   see also Children's Cancer
   Ward, oncology
capitalism 25, 109
Center for Development and
   Integration 185
Centers for Disease
   Control 120, 200
Chad 46, 50
charity 78, 100, 101n1
children 13, 59, 67, 84, 93–6,
   137, 141–5, 185, 190
Children's Cancer Ward 93–6
Chile 24, 164, 166, 171–2, 175–8
China 47, 50–1, 59–61, 150,
   162, 186
   see also Wuhan
church 96–7
class 82, 86, 88, 110, 121

climate change 2, 28, 68–9, 113, 197
Cold War 25
Colombia 164, 165, 175, 177
colonialism 43, 77, 82
Communist Party 181
Conservative Party 107
Corporate Social Responsibility (CSR) 77–89, 90, 90n1, 200
counselling 135, 144, 145
COVID-19
  antibodies 39
  Delta 182, 187, 191, 192
  fourth wave 38, 182, 186–9, 191
  Omicron 67, 105, 157, 189–90, 192
  second wave 65, 138, 139, 151, 183
  testing 38, 134, 156, 176, 181–4, 187, 191
  third wave 38, 139, 151, 183, 186
  transmission 96, 100, 139, 150–7, 183–4, 189
  variant 1, 2, 9, 38, 67, 104, 105, 113, 118, 119, 121, 125, 157, 182, 189–92
COVID-19 Vaccines Global Access Facility (COVAX) 60–6, 68, 97, 98, 125, 186, 192
Covishield 60
curfew 152, 156, 187
cybercrime 97

D

death 1, 9–11, 17, 18, 27, 38, 39, 47, 82, 86, 97–8, 110, 137, 151, 157, 163, 164, 182, 185, 187, 189–92
  see also infant mortality
debt 25, 26, 40, 44, 47, 52, 109, 111, 113, 154, 162, 179
democracy 12, 13, 25, 82, 86, 162, 171, 177, 178
Democratic Republic of the Congo 50, 51, 99

denialism 16
developing countries 40–2, 79
Development Studies Association Ireland (DSAI) 4
disability 1, 2, 9, 10, 89, 144
drought 154
Dyson 83

E

early treatment 9, 14–16
Economist Intelligence Unit 178
economy 15, 24–8, 40, 43, 51, 78–80, 89, 108–12, 150–5, 163, 176, 181–93, 197
Ecosavers Youth Network (EYN) 143
Ecuador 164, 167, 172, 177
education 18, 41, 42, 46, 52, 83, 84, 100, 138, 141
  see also school
El Salvador 164, 167, 171, 172, 177
employment 27, 31, 32, 40, 77, 78, 83, 84, 87, 88, 95, 96, 100, 112, 136, 139, 177, 182–8, 190
  see also unemployment
environment 10, 15, 28, 77, 78, 90, 90n1, 94, 95, 113, 124, 141, 142, 145
epidemiology 56, 67, 170
Equatorial Guinea 46, 51
ethical standards 77
Ethiopia 48, 50–1, 98–9
Eurobond 47
European Commission (EC) 66
European Union (EU) 26, 58, 66

F

farming 142, 144
financialization 108–10, 114, 199
fire 17
First World War 82
food 31, 82, 131–9, 140–2, 155, 183, 185, 187, 188
  banks 106
  see also hunger

Forbes 26, 108
foreign aid 40, 44
foreign direct investment
    (FDI) 39, 41, 44–7, 51
free-market economy 80
Friedman, Milton 24, 104,
    117–19, 122, 123
Fukuyama, Francis 25
furlough 28, 83

G

G7 Summit 65
gender 4, 26, 82, 86, 110, 139,
    140, 142, 145
Ghana 47, 48, 51, 64
Global Alliance for Vaccines and
    Immunisation (GAVI) 60–1,
    64
global financial crisis (GFC) 25,
    109, 111
Global Health Centre 121
globalization 25, 80
Global North 1, 3, 61, 68, 69,
    100, 105, 106, 112, 149
Global South 1–5, 10, 12, 24, 68,
    104, 105, 112, 191, 198, 199
God 28, 97, 132
Great Depression 25, 27
greed 104, 199
gross domestic product (GDP) 26,
    32, *43*, 46, 80, 99, 112,
    154, 189

H

handwashing 95, 96, 100, 138,
    144, 152
Hanoi 187, 190, 192
healthcare 1, 3, 16, 25, 28, 30,
    42, 44, 46, 64, 81, 82, 95, 99,
    100, 101n1, 106–10, 112, 135,
    190, 198–9
Health Impact Fund (HIF) 124
health worker 27, 56, 57, 126,
    136, 143, 182
high-income countries (HIC) 57,
    59, 65, 121

Hinduism 29, 79, 80
HIV 68
    see also AIDS
Ho Chi Minh City 187–8
Honduras 164, 168, 172, 175, 177
hospital 18, 31, 38, 84, 85, 88,
    93–5, 99, 100, 101n1, 107,
    134, 137, 187, 192
human rights-based approach 9,
    131–3, 200
hunger 31, 137
hydroxychloroquine 14–15

I

immunity 59, 65, 126
India 2, 10, 25–9, 30–2, 56, 60,
    61, 64–8, 77–90, 123, 131,
    135, 136, 163
    see also Odisha
industrialization 43, 181
inequality 1, 13, 25–7, 46, 56–9,
    61, 65–8, 86, 88, 104–14, 188,
    197, 199
infant mortality 46, 99
influenza 93, 134, 183
infodemic 15
insurance 29, 85, 139, 188
intellectual property 68, 114, 123
International Monetary Fund
    (IMF) 28, 40–2, 47, 67, 79,
    104, 111
International Organization for
    Standardization (ISO) 85, 90n3

J

Japan 58
Johnson & Johnson 58, 60, 65
Johnson, Boris 105

K

Kenya 48, 98, 99
Keynesianism 24, 28, 32

L

Latin America 17, 162–79

Lehman Brothers 25
liberalization 39, 40, 42, 80, 106
lockdown 27, 31, 86, 135, 136,
    138–40, 145, 149–58
    see also social isolation
low- and middle-income countries
    (LMICs) 66, 93, 96–9, 113
low-income countries (LICs) 56,
    106–7, 121

M

Magufuli, John 96–8
Mahatma Gandhi National Rural
    Employment Guarantee Act
    (MGNREGA) 31–2
Majaliwa, Kassim 96
manufacturing 30, 40–2, *43*, 50,
    51, 58, 67, 85, 100, 122–6,
    184, 187
manufacturing value added
    (MVA) *43*
mask 83, 85, 94, 96, 100, 136,
    140–4, 153–7, 190
Médecins Sans Frontières
    (MSF) 68
medication 16, 84, 114, 183, 199
Mexico 61, 163–4, 168, 172, 173,
    175, 177
Middle East 197
migrant 31–2, 82–3, 86, 106, 110,
    135, 136, 139–44, 184–5, 188,
    191, 193
Ministry of Corporate Affairs 81
Ministry of Health 14, 190
misinformation 9–17
Mission Shakti 136
Moderna 58, 65, 107, 122
money 29, 40, 86, 87, 109,
    118, 138
mosque 96–7
Mozambique 51, 99

N

national health system 9
    see also public health system
National Response Plan 183

natural disaster 134
necropolitics 9–18, 199
neoliberalism 11, 24–9, 30–2,
    40–4, 52, 79, 89, 104–9, 113
Nicaragua 164, 168, 170–3,
    175, 177
nongovernmental organizations
    (NGO) 4, 84, 93, 131–6, 137,
    139, 145

O

Odisha 131–45
    State Disaster Management
    Authority 135
oil 46, 144, 162, 179
oncology 101n1
Operation Warp Speed 58, 120
Organisation for Economic Co-
    operation and Development
    (OECD) 44–6
overmedicalization 16
overseas development aid
    (ODA) 44–5
Oxfam 24–7, 107, 184
Oxford University 59–60
oxygen 30, 38, 83, 84, 107

P

panchayat 135–6, 142, 144
Paraguay 164, 168, 172, 177
Patriotic Front (PF) 157
People's Cultural Centre
    (PECUC) 131, 137–9,
    141, 142–5
personal protective equipment
    (PPE) 38, 57, 83, 93, 96, 107
Peru 163, 164, 168, 172
Pfizer 58, 65, 107, 122, 186
pharmaceutical 1, 2, 16, 38, 42,
    61, 80, 85, 104, 107, 108, 113,
    117–26
Philippines, the 16, 186
police 82, 134
policymaking 1, 3, 4, 79, 80, 90
politics 11–18, 27, 105, 117, 162,
    177, 179, 199

population 4, 10, 15, 18, 25, 39, 64–9, 80, 86, 90, 101, 105, 110, 118–21, 125, 135, 137, 139, 152, 154, 177, 181, 185, 186–92, 198

populism 10, 11, 16, 178
  reactionary 11

post-truth 11–12

poverty 26, 38, 46, 69, 83, 86, 88, 90, 110, 124, 132, 138, 144, 163

prime minister 82, 86, 96, 165, 170, 182

privatization 24, 30, 42, 50, 80

profit 17, 26, 28, 39, 78, 80, 88, 90, 106–10, 113, 117, 120–7

public distribution system (PDS) 141–4

public health system 9, 13, 16–18, 29, 30, 192, 193

public spending 41, 99, 107

Q

quarantine 84, 87, 96, 134–6, 139, 140, 155, 176, 181, 187

R

racism 11, 27

Ramaphosa, Cyril 67

Randomised Evaluation of Covid-19 Therapy (RECOVERY) 14

recession 106

research and development (R&D) 58, 118, 120, 121

restaurant 155, 190

retail 136, 138, 140, 155, 184

rice 144, 185

rioting 176

Russia 59, 65
  see also Soviet Union

Rwanda 49, 98, 99, 156

S

sanitizer 83, 85, 87, 96, 100, 144, 153, 156

sarpanch 135–6

school 82, 94, 96, 138, 141, 144, 155, 183, 190

science 3, 4, 10–16, 197

Second World War 24, 83, 106

self-help group (SHG) 135–42

self-isolation 137, 183

Serum Institute of India (SII) 30, 60, 64, 65

severe acute respiratory syndrome (SARS) 9, 62, 183

sexism 27

Seychelles 39, 47, 49

shops   see retail

Sinovac 59, 61, 65

Sistema Único de Saúde (SUS) 1, 9–11, 16, 18

Smith, Adam 117

social distancing 156, 176, 183–6

socialism 109

social isolation 15–16

social media 10, 11, 15, 139, 175
  see also Twitter

South Africa 44–9, 97, 123, 156

South East Asia 181

South East Asian Games 191

South Korea 43, 58

Soviet Union 25, 79

Spanish flu 82

Special Drawing Rights (SDRs) 111–12

Sputnik V 60, 65

stay at home 27, 138, 152, 156

stock market crash 162, 179

Stranded Workers Action Network (SWAN) 31

Sub-Saharan African (SSA) 42–51

Sudan 46, 50, 51

sugar 50, 144

swine flu (H1N1) 57

T

Tanzania 49, 94–9, 100, 101n1, 157

tax 24, 26, 28, 39, 40, 52, 163, 185
  avoidance 39, 52, 68, 69, 106, 107, 112, 199

television 139, 143, 166–9
Test and Trace 107
  see also track and trace
tobacco 87, 138, 142–5
tourism 184, 190
track and trace 108, 176
Trade-Related Aspects of
  Intellectual Property Rights
  (TRIPS) 68
trade union 175, 185
travel 96, 121, 140, 152,
  155, 182–9
  international 155, 183–4
  restrictions 152, 184
Trump, Donald 16
Twitter 12

U

Uganda 98–9, 156
Ukraine 2, 41, 106
underdevelopment 198
unemployment 27, 40, 47, 88,
  112, 184, 188
United Nations Children's Fund
  (UNICEF) 65, 99, 120–6, 143
United Nations Conference
  on Trade and Development
  (UNCTAD) 41–6, 51
United Nations Development
  Programme (UNDP) 99, 188
United Party for National
  Development (UPND) 157
United States (US) 3, 16, 40, 56,
  65, 79, 106, 120–1, 163, 186
urbanization 181

V

vaccination *see* vaccine
vaccine
  booster 56, *63*, 67, 121, 190
  diplomacy 13, 192, 197–9
  inequality 56–69
  mRNA 58, 65
  nationalism 57, 105–6
  refusal 13

rollout 179
  trial 57–8, 68, 186
V-Dem 178
vegetables 136–42
Venezuela 164, 169, 173, 173,
  175, 177
victim 13, 83
Vietnam 181–93
  see also Hanoi, Ho Chi
  Minh City
violence 82, 139
volunteer 3, 94, 135, 141,
  189, 200
vulnerability 1, 4, 5, 10, 66, 69,
  82, 83, 86, 106, 111, 123,
  132–9, 184, 185, 188, 191,
  198

W

Walmart 83
war 24, 25, 41, 81–3, 106, 126,
  166–9, 197, 200
Washington Consensus 24
water 50, 78, 96, 142, 143
welfare 18, 26, 28, 39, 80, 84,
  135, 137
well-being 2, 13, 86, 89, 131
women 3, 27, 133, 135–44, 200
World Bank 40, 42, *43*, 45, *63*,
  67, 79, 99, 120, 182
World Earth Day 142, 145
World Food Programme 140
World Health Organization
  (WHO) 3, 15, 59, 67, 95, 110,
  120, 134, 149, 186, 200
World Trade Organization
  (WTO) 67, 68, 79
Wuhan 162

Y

Young Warrior programme 143

Z

Zambia 47, 49, 51, 98, 99,
  149–58